MW00696247

WHY WE

create

Reflections
on the Creator,
the Creation,
and Creating

EDITED BY

JANE CLARK SCHARL
AND BRIAN BROWN

SQUARE HALO BOOKS

In Christian art, the square halo identified a living person
presumed to be a saint. Square Halo Books is devoted to publishing
works that present contextually sensitive biblical studies and
practical instruction consistent with the Doctrines of the Reformation.
The goal of Square Halo Books is to provide materials
useful for encouraging and equipping the saints.

©2023 Square Halo Books, Inc.
P.O. Box 18954 | Baltimore, MD 21206
www.SquareHaloBooks.com

For information about the Anselm Society,
visit AnselmSociety.org.

All Scripture quotations unless otherwise labeled are from the
Holy Bible, English Standard Version®, copyright ©2001 by Crossway,
a publishing ministry of Good News Publishers. Used by permission.
All rights reserved. ESV Text Edition: 2011

Scripture quotation labeled KJV are from the King James Version of the Bible.

ISBN 978-1-941106-28-0
Library of Congress Control Number: 2023930992

All rights reserved. No part of this book may be reproduced without permission
from the publisher, except by a reviewer who may quote brief passages in a
review; nor may any part of this book be reproduced, stored in a retrieval system
or transmitted in any form by any means (electronic, mechanical, photocopying,
recorded or other), without permission from the publisher.

Printed in the United States of America

contents

PART 1

GOD CREATES

PART 2

WE CREATE

PART 3

GOD MEETS US IN CREATION

"Human vocation
is to reflect the love
and power of God
into the world,
and to reflect the
praises of the world
back to God."

N.T. WRIGHT[1]

Whose Story Are We Telling?

JESSICA HOOTEN WILSON

No one thinks a person a fool who takes a compass and map into the wilderness. We would recommend such aids. Better yet, stick to the trail. Many a fairy tale has warned the travelers not to stray from the path. While we encounter few protests in following standard guidance for going on a journey, if we transition from the literal to the metaphorical pilgrimage of life, suddenly there is a clamor of outrage: how dare you show me the way? Who made you the mapmaker? What if I believe that way is north?

Dante included all of us on his journey in the opening lines of his *Divine Comedy*, the poem that moves us from the lost woods to the heavenly city. Rather than singling out himself, he writes, "Midway along the journey of *our* life." Although Dante is the only pilgrim in the fictional tale, he suggests from the start that we all share this road by analogy. Each of us are pilgrims on our way.

We see this trope throughout literature: *The Divine Comedy, Canterbury Tales, The Road*. It is revealed to us in Scripture: the Israelites moving from wilderness to the promised land; Jesus's road to Calvary; the disciples called to Judea, Samaria, and to the ends of the earth.

Yet, we have all become like Alice in Wonderland, who asks for directions without caring which way to go or how she gets there:

> "Would you tell me, please, which way I ought
> to go from here?"
> "That depends a good deal on where you want to
> get to," said the Cat.
> "I don't much care where—" said Alice.
> "Then it doesn't matter which way you go."

The conundrum portrayed in this nineteenth-century children's story suggests a universal and timeless problem that has only intensified for contemporary Christians. We've lost our trust in those who know the directions, who have seen the map, and who could show us how to get home.

In her essay in this collection on memory, Heidi White quotes David Hicks, who suggests, "A good myth, like a good map, enables the wanderer to survive, perhaps even to flourish, in the wilderness." But we cannot devise such myths *ex nihilo*. As Peter Leithart and Matthew Clark show us, we are subcreators. We require stuff from which to create. If we are to tell the good stories of who we are and where we are going—if we are to follow the maps—we need the myths of the past. With the collective wisdom from the dead, we are piecing together a fuller picture of the landscape and our place in it.

Unfortunately, the Protestant Church is as leery of the imagination as it is of tradition, two compasses of the past that seem tainted and no longer functioning in the twenty-first-century world of science and ingenuity. Yet Dorothy L. Sayers differentiates poetic truth from scientific truth and demands we not ascribe the rubric of the latter to the former. The Book of Genesis, for instance, "was a book of poetic truth" and not a science manual, she argues. Had those in the controversy over evolution thought "of God as a great, imaginative artist—then they might have offered a quite different interpretation of the facts" presented by science, without being afraid that such facts disproved revelation.[1]

From Sayers's perspective, Genesis teaches us one incontrovertible fact about ourselves: we are made in the image of a Creator. If we want to know which direction is north, Sayers points us to our nature as creative beings. She writes, "The characteristic common to God and man is apparently that: the desire and ability to make things."[2] Just as Russian philosopher Nikolai Berdyaev says, "God created the world by imagination," so human beings think in images; our knowledge is imaged forth when we create imagined things.[3] In Brian Brown's words, God's Great Story begins at creation, and we retell this story when we too create. Through our creating, we show God's nature as Creator to be true.

"Surely an Act of the Imagination/ Helps more than one of Faith/ When a doubt brushes us," writes the great twentieth-century Catholic poet Elizabeth Jennings. In her poem

"Act of Imagination," Jennings walks through the mysteries of the creed: incarnation, crucifixion, resurrection, and how she desires for those ideas to become images. She longs for George Herbert's sonnets and Giotto's paintings to move her heart to God. Through these creative works, she touches Christ, she writes. At the end of the poem, Jennings exclaims, "Let faith be loud/ with the best imagining we have...." For by imagination, the invisible becomes tangible.

Our doctrines require imagination as much as orthodoxy requires tradition. We cannot entertain the creed in our minds and hearts without the particulars of the story of the God-Man. Nor can we be faithful followers without adhering to the authority of that history. Sayers asserts,

> Let us, in heaven's name, drag out the divine drama from under the dreadful accumulation of slipshod thinking and trashy sentiment heaped upon it, and set it on an open stage to startle the world into some sort of vigorous action.[4]

For Sayers, the dogma is the drama; orthodoxy is exciting, offensive, and compelling. Notice how both Jennings and Sayers share a communal imperative: "Let." Like Dante, these writers assume they are not writing to themselves but that their words are coming alive in the mind and heart of a reader. And because these readers are human beings, created in God's image, they are stirred by similar desires. These women act as guides, new Virgils that encourage pilgrims to continue on the way; new Isaiahs repeating God's call, "Come now, let us reason together" (Isaiah 1:18); new image bearers creating ways for us to touch Christ.

If it is true that we are made in another's image, then trying to write your own story, make your own way, follow your own path is as foolish as walking off into the wilderness without any tools. You are acting against your nature. So too is the Christian who rejects art, literature, history, and theology and assumes that he alone will find his way to God. It is like that joke where the drowning man refuses the assistance of the rowboat and emergency helicopter as he waits for God to save him. We must cultivate, to borrow Grace Olmstead's verb from her essay, a vision in which we can see the grace that God has created for us to know Him. Why walk blindly in the dark when God has presented us with so many lights?

Many people know the story of C. S. Lewis's conversion to Christianity, especially the part played by J. R. R. Tolkien. Apparently, the two (along with Hugo Dyson) stayed up one night arguing about the myth of the dying God. Afterwards, Lewis wrote to his friend Arthur Greeves (October 18, 1929), "Now the story of Christ is simply a true myth: a myth working in the same way as others, but with this tremendous difference that it *really happened.*"[5]

For those who believe in Christianity, such a revelation may be lost on them. But woe to those Christians who fall for the fallacy of the unconverted Lewis, whom Tolkien addresses as "Misomythos" (myth-hater) in his poem about this same conversation. These myth-haters believe "myths were lies" and fall for "progressive apes,/ erect and sapient. Before them gapes/ the dark abyss to which their progress tends." One may visualize the future Sauron and his orcs in the young Tolkien's description. In contrast to those who despise myths are those who see themselves as "little makers," Tolkien calls us, made to image God in the world, to tell His story through the creative story of our lives.

For these faithful artists and creators, we learn to see the myth that is true as our map home.

Seeking Our Place
in the Created Order

BRIAN BROWN

J. R. R. Tolkien's short story "Leaf By Niggle" tells the story of Niggle, an ordinary fellow who just wants to finish a painting. Over time, he is constantly distracted by the requests of his neighbors, and eventually he grows sick and dies, leaving his painting unfinished. As he navigates the afterlife, he finds that much of his character is judged by how he navigated the "distractions," which were not really distractions at all—but also that in both the world he left behind and the world ahead, the portion of the painting he did complete (a single leaf) had greater significance than he realized.

More than once, I've discussed this story with friends who nodded sagely and observed, "Yes, the moral of the story is that the ordinary things—the 'distractions'—are what really matters in life."

But I don't think that's what Tolkien hoped his readers would glean from his story. I think what Tolkien wanted to explore was something deeper.

That there are no ordinary things.

Many modern-era Christians have struggled to find their place in God's story, to understand how their vocations, the things that make them come alive, connect to their faith. Many have labored in frustration in church settings that had no answer to their questions of whether their work mattered. They live in a two-chapter story that begins with a sinner and ends with a trip to heaven (fall and redemption). And in such a story, everything hinges on the ending.

But as Tolkien knew, the Scriptures—God's own telling of the Great Story—do not have two chapters. The story includes fall and redemption. But it ends with a Restoration of God's created world—the consummation of something laid out at the very beginning, at Creation. If we miss the first and the fourth chapters, we miss the answers to two important questions. *What were we made for? And how then shall we live?*

To answer *those* questions, everything depends on the beginning. What is this place we live in, why is it here, and why are *we* here? What precisely did the fall sicken or damage, and how will it be restored to its fullness?

As the Anselm Society has labored toward its mission— a renaissance of the Christian imagination—we've seen the absence of this beginning hurting so many people's stories, whether they recognize it or not. Impeded creativity. Clouded vocational direction. Bitterness toward the Church. Susceptibility to trendy ideologies that present themselves to the church wrapped in favorite Bible verses and ask so much less of it than orthodoxy does. And the lie that goodness, truth, and beauty are separate menu options rather than a trinity.

But when you spend time with the Creation chapter of the story, answers start to fall into place to so many of the hardest questions that plague people day to day. Questions about purpose and identity, the relationship between Christian-ish activities and everything else, about how to navigate that whole "in the world but not of it" conundrum. More importantly, if you're properly formed by the entire four-chapter story, you begin to actually develop a Christian imagination—not just answers to isolated questions. You see the world differently: the way those people you *wish* you were more like see it.

The resources for such formation are well known in the Church, at least historically; our ancestors had many hundreds of years to figure them out. But in our particular time, some things have been forgotten that the Church should have been at pains to remember—and they need to be retold.

But not enough people have time to read the dozen or more books I and others could recommend to explore the Creation chapter properly. So our solution, as a starting point to serve our own community in Colorado (and perhaps others beyond it), was to go to the writers of those books and ask them to contribute to this introduction, this primer, this crash course in the Creation story. If you can't read a dozen books, perhaps we could create just one. Our hope is that this reading will be a beginning, a doorway into a larger world, a larger story—and a longer conversation.

That conversation begins with the Creation story itself. Read carefully, for every word here has meaning.

THE CREATION STORY

"There is one Almighty God, who made all things by
His Logos, both visible and invisible; [and] by the Logos,
through whom God made the creation, He also bestowed
salvation on the men included in the creation."
—Irenaeus of Lyon

In the beginning was God, Father, Son, and Holy Spirit, a
hierarchy of mutual love who was the perfect form of everything
good and true and beautiful.

And this one God burned with a divine redemptive purpose.

He looked into the disordered nothing, and He spoke
meaning—extending His nature to create matter reflecting that
nature. The light and the dark, the heavens and the earth, the land
and sea, the birds and fish, the plants and creatures. The Creator
was like a great tree at the center of everything, with everything
springing from it, dancing around it, swirling out and in, the Great
Dance going around and around, up and up. The heavens and
earth reflected the glory, the character of God. To look at the loving
hierarchies of His world, the diverse harmonies, the purposeful
ecosystems and thriving, was to see the character of the *Logos*
Himself, the Son, by whom all things were made.

And the Lord looked at this glorious dance and saw that it
was good, but it was not complete. It wanted a dance master, a
priest, to order and direct it toward its fullness and purpose as
God Himself did.

And so He created something new, something like Himself, something containing a part of Himself, spanning the gulf between Creator and created, between spirit and material. It would embody God's nature on the earth. It would be filled with His divine inspiration. It would participate not only in His work but in His very life. It would not merely follow its nature, trundling along and reflexively reflecting a small aspect of God's; it would willingly and creatively join the Logos in His work, because it would be filled with His spirit. It would see as God sees, not just the material things, but the spiritual realities to which they pointed, and in which they participated, so that it could incarnate the delights of God.

This species would be male and female, reflecting the diverse unity and self-giving ordered love of the Trinity in its very nature, as well as the relationship between the Creator and His creation. Its members would teach each other both to reflect His nature and to practice their own responsive purpose within it. For in what would almost seem an abomination, the Creator *made a place for humanity in His own redemptive creativity.* He was the beginning and the end, the initiator and the completor, but He gave to humanity a middle role, which it did not yet fully understand: that of worship.

Humanity would make the cosmos reverberate with the Creator's praises, as it filled and mobilized the entire planet with the quietest loves to the grandest endeavors, to reflect the beauty and harmony of God's divine nature. Humanity was made God's viceroy, His steward on the earth, and given authority given to no other creatures. Their place from the beginning of this Great Story was to do as God does, in His name, by His power, for His glory.

To fulfill this role, humans were given creative powers and duties; among them:

To cultivate. To love each person and each created thing in its proper way, learning and embodying the never-ending love of the Creator, willing the goodness of those given to their charge to see everything, not merely as it is but as it could grow to be. And in this, they would echo in a limited way the vision of the Creator who gave everything a nature and a purpose grander than it could imagine.

To name. To discern the meaning and design of each thing on earth, to name it for what it was and dedicate it to its Creator's glory, with His authority and His creative power. Not to name with recklessness or willfulness, not to seize the role of initiator, but to honor a thing for its true purpose. The power to name was a creative power, but it carried with it a duty to truth and goodness and meaning to the Creator Himself.

To subcreate. The humans' God-inspired genius would take grapes that God had made and make wine, take wheat and make bread. Their imitation of the Creator would make the very stones cry out the glory of God as cathedrals. They would take food, the building blocks of survival for every other creature, and make it a feast that would anticipate the marriage supper of the lamb.

And it was this last creative power, the power to take the second of three acts in God's redemptive purpose, that would be the thread followed by the remainder of the story.

OUR STORY WITH GOD
IN THE CREATION

This, my friends, is the Creation Myth. Not myth in the sense of falsehood, but in the sense of a story designed to communicate meaning and origins. It's the first chapter of God's Story. It tells in dramatic fashion our relationship to the Creator, the creation, ourselves, and each other. And it lays the groundwork for each of us to seek the answers to our individual questions. Who am I? What am I for?

We shouldn't have to experience it in so theologically dense a way; we should be able to experience it in pieces, repetitively, letting it soak in over time. But we've been so starved of much of the meaning in this story that you probably noticed a ton of things in the last section that made you think, *If that's true, that's really important.* (Or, *If that's* not *true, this is really dangerous.*) And many of them were probably ones you've never heard in church. The first time I told the Creation story this way verbally, it wasn't even quite as dense as what you see above, but I asked the audience to keep count of those exclamation mark moments. People counted as many as forty.

The rest of this book will unpack the major themes in that story, because they *are* incredibly important.

Because in this version of the story, the Fall means a bit more—a rejection of a very important created purpose and indeed God's own presence; a disordering of Creation; and the beginning of a long history of taking created, material things and either worshipping them, desecrating them, or creating evil things with them to draw glory to ourselves.

And Redemption means more than getting into heaven. Christ doesn't just suddenly appear in the story in Matthew; He, the Logos, cuts across time. The Incarnation is the Logos becoming one with humanity, giving it the power it did not possess in its fallen state, to do what it had been made to do: take its part in a threefold cycle of making creation glorify and indeed join the Creator.

This cycle is absolutely crucial to both redemptive history and our calling today, and it was in the DNA of this world from its inception. He would make wheat and we would make bread. He would make grapes and we would make wine. And He would make in the bread and the wine our homecoming, our reuniting with the Spirit whose presence we were made for.

In that promised unification, we would be called back to join in the work of stewardship and restoration, cultivating and creating and celebrating, and yes, mourning—as God does for things not yet fully healed—with a story that ends not in an untouched, wild land, or the beginnings of a garden, but in a holy city—in which our labors in the here and now matter for eternity, in which the culture that we make, in the words of Andy Crouch, "is the furniture of eternity."

For this is the chapter we find ourselves in, the chapter of Restoration, in which when all hope seemed lost, the storyteller has entered the story and has called His people to reunite with Him and enact the last chapter of the story.

THE BEGINNING

As I said, the rest of this book explores key themes from the Creation story, with the goal of illuminating for you this threefold dynamic:

God creates.

We subcreate.

God takes our subcreation, perfects it, and uses it to bring us more into His presence.

While you may encounter many ideas that are new to you, if we have done our jobs right, you will not encounter ideas that are new to Christianity. The writers are wise people well-versed in what we call the Great Tradition, or orthodoxy—the ideas that have stood the test of time, and met with broad agreement (except perhaps on nuances) across historic Christian traditions, time, and place.

My hope for you is that, by being introduced to what C. S. Lewis called the Deep Magic from before the dawn of time, you might be able to see more clearly the world you've been placed in, and your role in it. It is not a role we can resist with that insidious word, *just.* "I'm just a mom." "I'm just an engineer." "I'm just a student." "That's just a myth." "It's just a leaf." "It's just some person."

Because as Niggle learned in Tolkien's story, there are no ordinary things.

As the Creation chapter of the Great Story reminds us, the entire human race was made in the image of God, to reflect His glory across the universe. And our imaginations are redeemed for this purpose. So that everything we are, everything we believe, everything we do from the great loves to the smallest details of our daily lives might do what it was made to do. To offer your everything to God, so that He can make it extraordinary, as part of His Story.

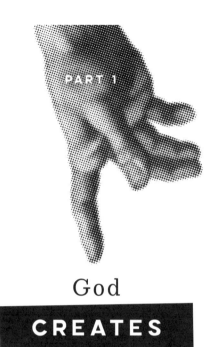

God

CREATES

The Relationship of Earth to Heaven

HANS BOERSMA

People have long made the mistake of believing either that this world is all there is, or that the next world is all that matters. But such a binary choice asks us to either ignore God or ignore His created order. Hans Boersma says that only by grappling with a third way can we truly come to know the Creator, His Creation, and what it means to be human.

In Plato's *Republic,* Socrates tells the story of a cave and of a group of people living in it. The people are seated facing the wall of the cave; behind them, a fire blazes; between the fire and the backs of their heads, many shapes are dancing, and the light of the fire throws shadows onto the cave wall. The people in the cave gape and wonder at the shapes on the wall; they believe that these shadows are ultimate reality and that there is nothing beyond them. Of course, that is not true; not only do the shadows on the wall merely mirror the shapes casting them, but the

shapes in turn simply mirror the true, real world, which exists
outside the cave.

This is how Nature, God's created order, can work. We see the
beauty of Nature, and we are drawn to it; we stare at it and study
it. All that is good. We should marvel at the world around us. But
like the people in the cave, we can make the mistake of believing
that this world—these beautiful shadows—are all there is. We
can come to love the created order *for itself* and make the mistake
of thinking the good things of the world are the best we can have.

An (equally erroneous) alternative to this mistake would be to
ignore the shadows, to close our eyes against them, and to refuse
to recognize that they are able to reveal truth to us—partial truth,
but truth nonetheless.

This second approach presents quite a challenge for people
whose occupations or passions are concerned with "this
world"—art, construction, science, indeed nearly every vocation
besides church ministry. They (or their friends) often struggle
to see their work as relevant and meaningful, both to God and
to people around them. How are they to avoid treating their
endeavors as meaningless, if this world is secondary to the next?

The two alternatives, however, need not be pitted against each
other as if they were the only two options—as if we had to choose
between the mistake of idolatry and that of indifference. When-
ever such a binary is given to us as a choice, we are asked to either
ignore God Himself or ignore His works. Neither can be right.

The world God has made is neither spiritually irrelevant nor spiritually ultimate. He made us for more than we have yet seen in this world—*and yet He placed us in it.* So, we must explore the nature of that world. It is only by grappling with the possibility of a third way that we come to understand what it means to be human.

This third way allows us to love the created order while not making it ultimate; it puts the created order in its proper place as a *theophany*—a *means of revealing God to us.* Only when we understand creation this way can we relate to it rightly. Only then can it serve us the way it was meant to.

Nature is not, in other words, going to be shoved aside to "make room" for Heaven. Instead, it is going to be transformed; it is going to fulfill its purpose of indicating, as fully as it was created to do, what really exists.

God gave us the gift of creation for us to glimpse truths, with our young eyes that cannot yet bear the true Light. The shadows on the cave wall truly intimate something of the shapes themselves, which in turn truly reveal some dimension of the reality outside the cave. The shadows deserve our attention—but not ultimately, for there is something beyond them that deserves more than our attention: it—or He Himself—deserves our deepest love.

So how are we to live in this beautiful shadow-world?

FURTHER UP . . .

J. R. R. Tolkien wrote a fairy tale about this (as did George MacDonald, Andrew Lang, Hans Christian Andersen . . . indeed, all fairy tales are about this in their own way), called "Smith of Wootton Major." It is a short story about a young man who is blessed, in a roundabout way, with a gift that grants him entrance into the land of Faery, where he sees and loves the created order more deeply than most of us do. As his peers grow up and abandon their childlike love of the created order for adult pursuits like wealth and power, Smith dwells with one foot in human society and one foot out—or rather, with one foot planted in the *created order* and one foot out. The story says,

> In Faery at first [Smith] walked for the most part quietly among the lesser folk and the gentler creatures in the woods and meads of fair valleys, and by the bright waters in which at night strange stars shone and at dawn the gleaming peaks of far mountains were mirrored. Some of his briefer visits he spent looking only at one tree or one flower; but later in longer journeys he had seen things of both beauty and terror that he could not clearly remember nor report to his friends, though he knew that they dwelt deep in his heart. But some things he did not forget, and they remained in his mind as wonders and mysteries that he often recalled.[1]

This is not some hidden pantheism of Tolkien's, nor is it merely a pretty tale. Smith encounters "wonders and mysteries," words we associate with the deeds of God, through God's created order (elevated to a level of dramatic strangeness through the title "Faery"); and these encounters "dwell deep in his heart." His encounters with the beauty of Nature change him; they transform him, and ultimately they ready him for the Great Encounter with Nature's maker Himself.

. . . AND FURTHER IN!

This is very different from the way many Christians have been taught to think about the relationship between Heaven and Earth, between the spiritual and the physical. Many of us have learned to think of Heaven (or the spiritual) as the most important, yet somehow less real, than the world of the senses (or the physical). Our faith tells us that Heaven is most important, while our observations inform us that Earth is more real.

Can it really be that we should give our allegiance to what is most important (Heaven), while nonetheless we claim that something is most real (Earth)? How do we deal with this tension? Let's explore in some detail what Scripture says about the heavenly Kingdom of God. The words used in the Bible function as hooks, if you will, to hang our imaginative impulses on as we try to embrace the reality that life does not end with death. That language is earthly, even earthy in places. It uses elements of the created order to give us a sense of what God's Country is like. Look at the Book of Revelation, where St. John receives a highly detailed, descriptive vision about the City of God. This vision is specific enough that it is possible to do a proportionate rendering of the City; the angel gives John dimensions and architectural specifications galore. John also provides other sensory details about the heavenly City: it smells of incense ("the prayers of the saints") and it resounds with beautiful music from harps.

God is showing us His Country using images that we can grasp: rivers, animals, cities, clouds, harps. It is clear from Scripture that Heaven is a weighty affair, heavy with reality and significance.

Of course, no one should think that in Heaven we will literally be playing harps while seated on clouds. But the "harps and clouds" language is there for a reason. The ethereal character of the imagery reminds us that we ought never be quite at home in the beautiful world we inhabit. Instead of working to make this world our ultimate home, we should strive to make ourselves at home in Heaven *now*. And instead of transposing Heaven into the world, we should use the world as God's gift that is meant to remind us of Heaven itself. Sometimes Christians speak about Heaven as simply a better Earth, a place where we will get to drink beer just like we do here, except that it will be *perfect* beer; where we will get to gather with friends and family, except that these will be *perfect* gatherings. Our lack of imagination makes us think of Heaven in purely natural terms.

That is not the real story at all. To go back to Plato's allegory of the cave, when the people in the cave begin to realize that the shadows on the wall are just that—shadows—they imagine the shapes casting the shadows as simply *better shadows.* That does not begin to get to the truth of the situation! The shapes themselves have a reality that the shadows do not: you can hold them and touch them. They have three dimensions, not just the two dimensions of the shadows. The shapes exist quite differently than the shadows they cast; the shadows do reveal something of the truth of the shapes (their outline, their size in relation to each other, etc.), but only in part. In Plato's allegory, there is even another layer of reality. The shapes, in turn, manifest something of the really-real things, which exist in the world outside the cave. To say that the world outside the cave, the world of sunlight and grass and water and mountains, is essentially a world of *even better shadows* would be laughable!

Heaven is not simply a world of better shadows. The Earth is beautiful because it is a world that manifests God. (The term *theophany* means "manifestation of God.") We dare not neglect God's good creation as something indifferent or bad. Neither, however, should we turn the physical world into an idol: once we join God and the saints, we see God's heavenly throne room itself. Heaven is a thing of more dimensions, more reality, and therefore more meaning than the Earth we experience today. From our experiences on Earth, we can begin to trace the outline of Heaven. But to fill in the outline, we have to wait till we're there. Only then will our longing be stilled and will we see Beauty itself.

CHRIST THE LIGHT

St. Athanasius, a Church Father who combated the heresy of Arianism, famously said, "God became man so that man might become god." This is a challenging assertion, one that might make many Christians recoil. That man might become *god?* How can we talk that way?

This assertion is more than poetic language. It is the whole crux of the relationship between Earth and Heaven. God created the natural world so that we, His image-bearers, could come to know Him in a unique way through the creation we see all around us. But we ruined that creation; through sin; we dragged it down from its theophanous aim. Now we vacillate between ignoring creation and worshiping it—and both responses are wrong.

God was not content to leave us to flounder blindly through the beautiful world He gave us. And to restore our vision, He sent the Light of Heaven into the created world, so that we might learn the truly godly way to relate to the gift of creation He has given us.

In the person of Christ, God Himself entered this world. God walked among the shadows, and taught us how to seek the realities. In Christ's life on earth, God participated in the activities of Earth: He talked, ate, worked, walked. He slept on a boat rocking on the waves. He loved gardens and mountains, like many of us do, for He returned to these scenes of nature throughout His ministry. He attended parties and contributed to the joy of them (think of the Wedding at Cana). We know from Christ participating in these things that they are good, that they have a genuine usefulness, that they are worthwhile. But they are not enough. They are not ultimate. They are not, in short, Heaven. And therefore they cannot give full satisfaction, for only God Himself satisfies our deepest desires.

The Incarnation gives us two mysteries. The first is that through Christ, God became man. This is the culmination of the downward movement begun at Creation: God coming down and giving Himself, first by making the heavens and the earth, and then by becoming embodied in the fullness of time.

But this is not the whole story; we must not lose sight of the other mystery: there is an upward movement as well, a return of the poured-out flood of God's creative love, in which God is drawing things back into His divine self. God is making all things—and especially humanity—divine.

This mystery was central to the early Church. The very first Christians placed great emphasis on Jesus's divinity; we modern Christians tend to focus on His humanity. Both are wholly true; but this shift in emphasis has a ripple effect on our whole conception of Christian living. The center of Christianity is that God is transforming us into Himself: He wants us to join the triune life; that is the deepest mystery of the Incarnation, of salvation itself.

HEAVEN HERE AND NOW

Let's go back to the allegory of the cave. In the story, Socrates tells of a person who realizes that the shadows on the wall are just that: shadows. He turns to find the source and sees behind him, backlit by crimson flames, the shapes themselves. He contemplates these for a long time, learning to understand and appreciate them; he learns to love them more than he loved the shadow, because they are closer to the truth.

If the created world is the shadow, the embodied Church is the shape: it is nearer the reality. Learning the stories and the teachings of the Church and allowing those things to shape our imaginations, our judgments, our day-to-day decisions, all these brings us closer to reality.

But God has given us something even better. Socrates tells of how, after learning to love the shapes, the person in the cave suddenly realizes that beyond the fire, there is a tunnel. There is a Way Out—and that means that there is a World Out, a whole different depth of reality that the shapes only indicate. So he begins to climb. The climb is difficult; he is not used to walking, as he has spent his entire life crouched before the wall of the shadows. He falls often, cutting his hands and knees on the rocks. He does not know where he is going. Behind him, he hears the mutterings of those he used to call his friends, those with whom he loved the shadows; none of them is stumbling or bleeding. But he presses on. And at last, he sees a Light: a Light like nothing he has ever even begun to imagine, a Light in which the brilliance of the flames would fade and become pale. He emerges from the cave, into the Real World, and for a long time he cannot see it because his eyes are simultaneously seared from the sun and blurred with tears.

Seeing Heaven is hard. But God gives us a way to do it. Alexander Schmemann, a well-known Orthodox theologian, writes in his classic book *For the Life of the World* that the liturgy is Heaven itself, is Paradise. When we step into Church, we step into Heaven. This may be hard to believe. But throughout Christian history, great saints have attested to this reality: Church is a unique glimpse of Heaven.

When Revelation talks of harps and clouds, it gives us a peek into eternal worship itself. In Revelation, Heaven is a never-ending liturgy, a never-ending chorus of praise to God. "Harps and clouds" are far from abstract or unreal. They are the very best, the most real of all things. They are the liturgical worship. And on Sunday mornings, we get a taste of this final glory, which is the worship of God.

Now, of course, harps and clouds are no more literal than heavenly beer or parties. Language about Heaven is always God accommodating Himself to us. Scripture uses the best that we know here to give us a sense of what Heaven will be; it is not telling us exactly what it will be. Harps and clouds are significant and weighty metaphors, for they tell us that Beauty itself—God in Christ—is the true and final reality. He alone satisfies the aching longing that throughout our lives we have felt.

A too-earthly imagination stunts our vision of Heaven. We must have heavenly imaginations—accepting that Heaven reaches beyond our earthly existence, for only the experience of otherworldly Beauty is worth sharing on Earth.

SACRAMENTAL CREATION

How, then, shall we live? How then shall we rightly and truly love the divine gifts of this Creation all around us, while also stretching our souls and our imagination towards heaven?

St. Paul reminds us that "our citizenship is in heaven" (see Philippians 3:20; also Ephesians 2:12), which means that our eyes must be fixed on another world. Earthly things place their rightful demands upon us. This world is not empty or worthless, something to be discarded. As Schmemann says,

> Christ came not to *replace* "natural" matter with some "supernatural" and sacred matter, but to *restore* it and to fulfill it as the means of communion with God. The holy water in Baptism, the bread and wine in the Eucharist, stand for, i.e. *represent* the whole of creation, but creation as it will be at the *end*, when it will be consummated in God, when He will fill all things with Himself.[2]

Nature is not, in other words, going to be swept aside so as to "make room" for Heaven. Instead, it is going to be transfigured. To return to our story of the cave once more, the shadows will be put in their proper relationship to reality. They will indicate, as fully as they were created to do, that which is really-real. That is why Schmemann speaks of creation "as it will be at the *end,* when it will be consummated in God, when He will fill all things with Himself."

When we think of the relationship between Earth and Heaven this way, it becomes clear how we are to live. Our lives on Earth, within this creation, have a two-fold purpose: we are meant to *act* to manifest God's grace in the world, and we are called to *contemplate* God's love in the liturgy, so as to shape our imaginations and accustom our eyes to Heaven itself.

In Plato's allegory, the man who leaves the cave spends many days walking about on the grass, staring up at the sky, marveling, rejoicing. He has found the really-real—Heaven itself, we might say. But eventually, he feels a tug in his spirit. He remembers his companions in the cave, those who stare at the shadows and love them wrongly—love them not as shadows but as ultimate truths. And so he makes the difficult decision to go back down, to bring word of what he has seen into the cave. This way, he hopes to help his companions realize the proper meaning of the shadows and shapes, so that his companions may begin their own journey toward the Light.

The lesson for Christians is simple but paradoxical: the more we love Heaven, the richer our lives here on Earth. Only by striving to participate in another world can we rightly engage with this one. In "Smith of Wootton Major," the most worldly character is also the laziest, the least engaged with fruitful human activity; the most otherworldly characters are the most active, whose many deeds shine out with excellence, because their hearts always seek Heaven.

We are called to seek Heaven always. That does not drive us to abandon this world; instead, it leads us to return time and time again to this world. Creation is good; it will be taken up into the divine life. We, as God's witnesses in this world, have a calling to participate in that upward motion. We are blessed to be able to bring things from this life into the divine Life itself. True, we walk through what C. S. Lewis called "the Shadowlands." But we need not walk in darkness. Wherever there is a shadow, there is also a light. And the heavenly Light directs us to itself, already on Earth.

Matter and Its Creator

PAUL BUCKLEY

What is Genesis 1 if not the prelude to God's utter delight in the mundane? Teacher and worship leader Paul Buckley notes that in the liturgy of creation, the recurring antiphon is "God saw that it was good." Six times. Who are we then not to take creation seriously?

God made all things good—so says the Book of Genesis— but one Sunday morning, I doubted that my "Bible-believing" congregation believed it. I mean really believed it with a Luther-like "Here I stand" tenacity. So I began my remarks with a diagnostic quiz.

"I'm going to quote a snippet from a song," I said. "Let's see who can finish it: 'And the things of earth . . . '"

The response was instant and unanimous: ". . . will grow strangely dim in the light of his glory and grace."

"Good," I said. "Now try another: 'This is my Father's world, he . . .'"

Crickets.

"This is my Father's world," I repeated, "he ..."

More crickets. At last, a lone voice from the back completed the line: "He shines in all that's fair."

"So which is it?" I wondered aloud. "One song says earth grows dim in the light of God's glory. The other says He shines in all that's fair."

It was clear which hymn formed our imaginations more, at least in my congregation—and I suspected this congregation was not alone. But which hymn got nearer the truth?

To be fair to Helen Lemmel, the hymnwriter responsible for "Turn Your Eyes Upon Jesus": maybe when she wrote that the "things of earth grow strangely dim," she didn't mean the glory-gilded gifts of creation. Maybe she meant something like "becoming a billionaire at 29 and facing a terminal prognosis at 30," a scenario in which even billions of billions of dollars and all the acclaim of humanity would indeed grow dim. It is odd, however, that "Turn Your Eyes Upon Jesus" differentiates so clearly between "the things of earth" and Christ's "glory and grace," especially when Scripture writers themselves do not draw such a stark line here.

As I told my congregation that morning, if I could sing only one line or the other as a way to sum up a creation credo, I'd keep Maltbie Babcock's *He shines in all that's fair.* (And if I could snag a second line from the same hymn: *He speaks to me everywhere.*)

After the sermon, a woman approached me, and it was clear that she ... disagreed. "The problem with that hymn," she said, swayed by the persistence of evil in the world, "is that this is not my Father's world."

The baldness of her denial surprised me, but the sentiment did not. I had long suspected that the congregation as a whole shared it. It's why I devoted a couple of months to talking about creation. Of course, neither this Christian woman nor anyone else in the church would deny that God made the world. But there was no robust sense that the things of earth are things of God, that they matter, and that He means to redeem them.

Christian faith is creation faith. The evidence is all around us that the Christian faith takes matter seriously. Every time we sing the Nicene Creed, we insist that matter matters—the matter of heaven and earth; the matter of the Virgin's womb; the matter of the Son's flesh, crucified and raised from death; the matter, in an age to come, of the resurrected dead. We baptize bodies with water. We share bread and wine. And yet many Christians seem uncomfortable with the sheer physicality of their faith. Instead of embracing it, they play it down. Theologians aren't immune; they can be among the least comfortable. "We all agree that water is necessary for ordinary baptism," writes the Orthodox theologian Alexander Schmemann, "but how often does one feel that a classical theologian really likes water, has ever really noticed what it is?"[1]

GLORY AND GRACE IN CREATION

The Scriptures, and Christian tradition at its healthiest, are far more enthusiastic about creation than your average American Christian. And creation talk amounts to more than a bare affirmation that God made things. It also says that the things God made tell us something about Him. The things of earth communicate something.

This isn't a uniquely theological idea. It's true on a human level too. The things we make and the work we do say something about us. So the creation, in every detail, reveals its Creator. One of the glories of being human is that we can learn to read that revelation both with our minds and with our imaginations.

"[Y]ou came to be for the sake of no other thing except that you be an instrument fit for the glory of God," St. Basil the Great wrote in the fourth century. "And for you this whole world is as it were a book that proclaims the glory of God, announcing through itself the hidden and invisible greatness of God to you who have a mind for the apprehension of truth."[2]

St. Basil practiced what he preached. In a way that one seldom finds in modern theological writing, he may on one page seek to explain "the image of God" and on the next ponder the habits of dolphins or vultures. He explores the meaning of human anatomy and human relationships. He reads the world. When Basil likens creation to a book, he stands on firm biblical ground. Scripture makes the point repeatedly: Creation testifies to its Creator. Psalm 19, which extols the perfections of the written Torah, says that the creation has a voice as well: "The heavens declare the glory of God, and the sky above proclaims his handiwork." Attentiveness to God's voice in the Scriptures is a nonnegotiable for Christians, but remarkably often those same Scriptures become a field guide pointing us to the world around. "Ask the beasts, and they will teach you," says Job. "Go to the ant," says Solomon. Look at the birds and consider the lilies, says Jesus.

When we talk about God's glory in creation, it's tempting to reduce the idea to beauty: A beautiful sunset reminds us of the beauty of God. It's true, but more than beauty is on display. According to St. Paul, God's "invisible attributes, namely, his eternal power and divine nature, have been clearly perceived, ever since the creation of the world, in the things that have been made" (Romans 1:20). Of course Paul knows that human beings can turn a blind eye to clear things. They can plug their ears and sing nanny boo boo. A high school classmate once planted himself at the back of a room and reclined behind a desk, then groused that he couldn't hear. The teacher paused. "Lean forward," she said, and went on with her lecture. A slouching, unappreciative back-of-the-room complainer—that's not a bad image of recalcitrant humanity. Basil and a host of other saints urge us: Lean forward. See what the poet Gerard Manley Hopkins saw: "The world is charged with the grandeur of God."

When we say that the God who spoke creation into existence speaks through it still, we are not ignoring the truth that He has spoken most fully through the person of His Son. In fact, we need that revelation in Jesus to read creation well. Jesus is the

Word through whom all things were made; in Him is life (see John 1:1–4). By Him "all things were created, in heaven and on earth . . . all things were created through him and for him. . . . and in him all things hold together" (Colossians 1:15–20). The Son "upholds the universe by the word of his power" (Hebrews 1:3). When we engage creation, we do not engage a generic creator. We engage—and are engaged by—Jesus Himself, a Jesus who remains active within His creation.

Creation, then, is no less central to the New Testament than to the Old. The fourth and fifth chapters of Revelation allow us to see and hear and smell a heavenly liturgy. Here we might expect to find world-weary saints and martyrs for whom the things of earth, finally, really have grown dim. Instead, we see a band of white-robed presbyters casting crowns and giving glory to God for the things of earth and much else besides:

> Worthy are you, our Lord and God,
> to receive glory and honor and power,
> for you created all things,
> and by your will they existed and were created.
> (Revelation 4:11)

Creation is redeemed, not abandoned, because creation tells the story of God's glory in its own unique way.

LEARNING TO READ THE BOOK

Reading the book of creation isn't a matter of breaking a code
that leads us to a myriad of facile equations: a hedgehog means
x, a dandelion means y, a seahorse means z. Reading creation
isn't like looking up a word in the dictionary. It's more like
returning again and again to pore over a favorite poem by a
favorite poet, and always discovering more to savor. For a dictionary, you just need to know the alphabet. For the poem, you need
wisdom, a willingness to linger, imagination, and love.

And holy curiosity. I love the open-endedness of a line in
Psalm 8 that refers vaguely to "whatever passes along the paths
of the seas"—as if to say, I know there's more to creation than
we yet see; and Lord only knows what we'll find in Australia. "It
is the glory of God to conceal things, but the glory of kings is to
search things out" (Proverbs 25:2).

So let's try a little creation reading, with something simple,
like bread.

The Jewish physicist Gerald L. Schroeder likes to ask his
students what it takes to make bread. Their first answers center
on the ingredients, which couldn't be simpler: water, flour, yeast.
But there's a lot more—more of creation—that goes into a loaf.
You need soil and a favorable climate. You need "extraterrestrial
input" in the form of sunlight. You need a being who wants
bread in the first place and who can concoct a recipe, and who
has the savvy to reshape created matter into an oven. That rules
out wallabies and wildebeests and the like. This endeavor will

require human beings. "To make a loaf of bread you need a very special universe."[3]

Paul says that God is revealed "in the things that have been made" (Romans 1:20). Every bit of what goes into bread—not the ingredients alone but the whole history from grain to loaf—is something that has been made. So what does bread say? Better: What, through bread, does God say?

Raindrops fall. The sun shines. Both, says Jesus, are God's acts of kindness. He gives sun and rain, both to the just and to the unjust. Note that Jesus's point has an ethical application: These indiscriminate meteorological phenomena teach us to love enemies (see Matthew 5:44–45). Both water from above and light of the sun are needed for grain to grow. And both say: God is great, God is good, God is kind.

But before grain can grow, it has to die and be buried, before it can rise again. Speaking of His own impending execution, Jesus said, "Unless a grain of wheat falls into the earth and dies, it remains alone; but if it dies, it bears much fruit" (John 12:24). This is not merely a convenient figure of speech. Rather, God has woven into creation the pattern of death and resurrection. The harvest says God is the God who brings life out of death.

Bread-making takes time, another created reality that communicates to us about God's glory. It takes time for a grain of wheat to die in the ground and then to grow. It takes time to harvest. It takes time for yeast to work. It takes time to mix ingredients. It takes time to bake them. And all that time is good. I once complained to a friend that his ecclesiastical tradition needed to shape up soon. "And I'd like to plant an acorn today and have a nice big oak tomorrow," he said. "It's not how God made the world."

My friend was right. God Himself, from the beginning, took time. Being God, He could have said "Shazam!" and made it all in an instant. But God took His time with creation. He set up the world—dividing night and day, waters above and waters below, sea and dry land, and so forth—in stages. He willingly submitted to the passing of time (and not just at creation, but also in the incarnate Christ's life on earth). Each day was good, but the next was always more glorious. God's time-taking sets a pattern for human beings, and it shouldn't surprise us that our works—like bread making—take time. Bread says: The stuff of the world has a future; it will be transfigured, glorified, renewed.

Every loaf of bread, then, is far more than the sum of its ingredients. Imagine that moment when the Olive Garden waiter delivers a steaming breadbasket to your table. When you, salivating, peel back the waxed paper to unveil the garlic-buttery goodness within, what do you see? Just breadsticks? If you have eyes to see, you can see the whole world in a loaf of bread. You can see God's kindness, God's power over death, God's promise to make all things new.

Does that seem like more weight than a loaf of bread can bear? On the night He gave Himself up for the life of the world, Jesus went even further. He took bread in His hands, gave thanks, and said, "This is my body."

A certain kind of Christian would say all this talk about

bread—this exercise in reading a bit of creation—isn't very "spiritual." It seems awfully mundane to spend so much time reflecting on bread making. But what is Genesis 1 if not the beginning of God's utter delight in the mundane? Mundane means *of the world.* In the liturgy of creation, the recurring antiphon is "God saw that it was good." Six times. And a climactic seventh: "Behold"—a biblical *nota bene*—"it was very good." Good, in the creation story, doesn't mean just "okay," a quality one notch above "so-so" on a spectrum that moves on up to "better" and "best." As the ancient Greek translators of Genesis knew, it includes beauty. Light, the recurring cycle of evening and morning, palms and pines, sun, moon, and stars in their courses above, balletic whales and phosphorescent fish, furry things that walk on all fours, human beings, the complementarity of male and female, the stuff of bread—all good, all beautiful. All very good.

Psalm 104 is the greatest creation psalm. It reaches a climactic moment with this burst of praise:

> O Lord, how manifold are your works!
> In wisdom have you made them all;
> the earth is full of your creatures. (v. 24)

What on earth moves the poet to that exclamation? A lot of things. The psalm praises God's work in rivers and valleys, in wind and water. It rejoices in God's gifts to animals, even those far removed from ordinary human life—wild goats, rock badgers, lions, whales. And it celebrates bread making.

You cause the grass to grow for the livestock
and plants for man to cultivate,
that he may bring forth food from the earth
and wine to gladden the heart of man,
oil to make his face shine
and bread to strengthen man's heart. (vv. 14–15)

This is the thick creation faith that we need, especially at a
cultural moment such as ours, when even Christians are given
to despair. That worshiper who summarily deconstructed "This
Is My Father's World" one Sunday was actually reflecting an
age-old tension for many Christians. On one hand we hear that
"God so loved the world" (John 3:16). On the other we hear, from
the same biblical writer, "Do not love the world or the things in
the world. If anyone loves the world, the love of the Father is not
in him" (1 John 2:15). The second might seem at first glance to
undercut a view of creation that finds God shining and speaking
everywhere. But it becomes obvious that "the world" and "things
in the world" don't mean "God's good creation" and His "manifold
works." John himself clarifies that by "things in the world," he
means disordered loves: "the desires of the flesh and the desires
of the eyes and pride of life" (2:16). He doesn't encourage an
indifference to God's creative work.

Every psalm was written in what we call "the real world." And
every psalmist was a man of sorrows, acquainted with grief. As
the theologian Craig Bartholomew has said, "It wasn't easy being
Israel." Israel suffered, sometimes innocently, sometimes justly.

Israel was awake to evil, even its own. No biblical writer can be accused of naivete about the power of human beings to abuse, kill, and destroy. And Israel's worship offered no pie-in-the-sky escape from the ugliest realities. More than a third of the psalms are laments. "It is not well with my soul," they say, "or with the world." The Israelites were as attuned to evil as the woman who said, "This is not my Father's world."

But for all that realism about "the real world," the things of earth didn't grow strangely dim. Israel was too attuned to creation's song for that to happen. In the beginning was music. God called things into existence "by the breath of his mouth" (Psalm 33:6), and the "morning stars sang together" (Job 38:7). The creation is a thoroughly enchanted—*en-chant-ed: en-sung*—place. This insistence on the goodness and glory of creation is a big part of what made Israel Israel. In the worst of times, the wicked may "kill the widow and the sojourner, and murder the fatherless" (Psalm 94:6), and "my companions . . . become darkness." (Psalm 88:18) Nonetheless, and at all times and in all places:

> The earth is the Lord's and the fullness thereof,
> the world and those who dwell therein. (Psalm 24:1)

> In his hand are the depths of the earth;
> the heights of the mountains are his also.
> The sea is his, for he made it,
> and his hands formed the dry land. (Psalm 95:4–5)

Israel never surrenders its vision of an enchanted creation that chants back to God. Think of Psalm 148, which calls on all creatures great and small to praise the Lord. Psalm 96 summons the whole creation to sing:

Let the heavens be glad, and let the earth rejoice;
let the sea roar, and all that fills it;
let the field exult, and everything in it!
Then shall all the trees of the forest sing for joy before the
Lord,
for he comes, for he comes to judge the earth.
He will judge the world in righteousness,
and the peoples in his faithfulness. (vv. 11–13)

The whole created order rejoices in the hope that God will ultimately right all wrongs.

THE CROWN OF CREATION

Here I want to highlight something that has remained implicit, and it has to do with human beings. When we think of God's glory in creation, what images come to mind? What fills Christian posters and memes when the caption is, say, "The whole earth is full of His glory"? The images are typically what we call "nature scenes"—purple mountain majesties, sunsets, landscapes, seascapes, waterfalls, rainbows. What's missing in those photos of the glory of God? The image of God.

Last summer, my wife and I visited the Grand Canyon. Early one evening we squatted on a rock to watch the sunset and enjoy a romantic moment with a few dozen other people. There in the golden western sky was a panorama of God's glory. I tried repeatedly to capture it in a perfect photo—the "Christian poster" shot—but various specimens of the image of God kept getting in the way.

The Scriptures don't do that. Unlike me and unlike our posters, when they speak of God's glory filling the earth, they don't try to leave human beings out of the picture. We have seen that already in Psalm 104, in which even an ordinary workday becomes fodder for praise: "Man goes out to his work and to his labor until the evening" (v. 23). And there are plenty of other examples. Psalm 72, a prayer for the king, closes with a doxology that also serves to round out the second book of the psalter. The doxology blesses God and ends this way: "May the whole earth be filled with his glory! Amen and Amen!" What does the psalmist imagine that would look like? A depopulated aerial photo of the Grand Canyon? No. The psalm casts a vision of righteous rule. The good king defends the cause of the most vulnerable. He governs with justice. The psalmist prays for abundance of the fruits of the earth. And for this:

> And may people blossom in the cities
> like the grass of the field! …
> May people be blessed in him,
> all nations call him blessed! (Psalm 72:16–17)

Justice among human beings, worldwide blessing, people flourishing in cities—this is how the poet envisions an earth filled with God's glory: a creation crowned with God's image in humanity.

All to say: God's self-revelation in the created order isn't just "out there" at a distance in grand nature scenes. It's also up close and personal. God reveals Himself within and around human beings. St. Basil again: "Do not despise the wonder that is in you."[4]

Let us aspire to be a people who, of all people, know how to celebrate, with thanksgiving and worship toward the Creator, the goodness of creation and those things that are most truly human. One way to recalibrate our creation faith (if it isn't already obvious) is to sing the psalms and make them our own. Over and over, the psalms reorient us to the goodness of and hope for God's revelatory creation. They give us a way to sing, with full heart and full voice, a profound Amen to God's own judgment of His very good world. In the light of His glory and grace—the only light by which we'd want to see, or can—we may well find that the things of earth shine out, gloriously vivid.

Time and Its Creator

JANE CLARK SCHARL

*What if time is more than the passing of
moments? What if it's a gift to experience
Heaven now? We are, after all, "eternal in
God's eyes," as C. S. Lewis says. Jane Scharl
asks us to explore what a new understanding
of time reveals about our past and future,
about prayer, and about creating.*

Imagine this: a person, a woman, on her knees praying fervently.
All her being is present in the prayer. Her body is poised as if to
spring into action; her face is fixed, though her eyes are closed;
she is praying for a man, a relative of hers, who she knows
is enduring brutal torments. He is being burned alive. She is
praying for him, bringing all that she is to God to intercede for
this man, that he might have joy and steadfast hope, that after all
his tortures he would see salvation.

    Now imagine that the man had been burned to death four
hundred years prior. Yet the woman prays, and her prayer ascends,
and God hears, and four hundred years before the prayer is said, it

is answered. A soul is granted perseverance and is saved.

This is a remarkable scene, but not for the reasons we may think. It is remarkable because prayer is remarkable; nothing else. For those who have considered truly the nature of the God to whom we pray, time makes as little difference as space. If we do not hesitate to pray for a fellow human separated from us by half the globe, we ought not hesitate to pray for someone separated from us by such a trivial thing as time.

It may seem hubristic to call "time" a trivial thing. Few things have as much control over our day-to-day experiences as time. We even call the basic elements of our lives "day-to-day"; in other words, time mediates what we experience as the fabric of our lives. But let us follow that prayer upward, from the very instant (how all our language is ruled by time!) it comes into being in the heart, and see where it goes.

The woman—you, perhaps, or a friend of yours—sees or recalls or hears about some pain, some suffering elsewhere in this world. It seizes her and drives her to turn her mind toward God. The prayer begins as a voiceless cry, an inclining of the imagination toward the One and Three. Perhaps (it seems possible) this is the highest form of prayer: a wordless longing, an instinctive turning of the spirit and the will to God. I do not know. She, at least, is not content with this. She goes into her room hastily, closes the door, and falls to her knees. She buries her face in her hands clasped on the edge of the bed, and she begins to form thoughts, images, and finally words. She casts all these things desperately up and out, she knows not where. She prays for many minutes, ten, twenty, moving through words to silence and back again to words. In the space of this prayer, she labors; she is in agony, and she offers up all the energy and attention that she has to her plea. At last, she is exhausted. She says, "Thy will be done," and leans back on her heels. The world presses in around her, time and space alike. She has to get dinner in the oven. Her prayer is done.

But what do we mean, *Her prayer is done*? Isn't it more likely that the prayer has just begun? That when the woman rises and goes about her day, attending to the tasks that demand her immediate attention, giving her love to the little things crowding around her, her prayer continues to resonate in eternity, calling out for the Almighty's ear?

Now, imagine that four hundred years before, the man burning in agony on the pyre cries out, begging for relief, for hope. Does not his cry too hang in eternity? So what do we call the instant in eternity (which does not consist of instants) where his cry meets her intercession?

DESCENDING AND ASCENDING

Full disclosure: I have not invented this scene. It is central to the novel *Descent into Hell,* by Charles Williams, one of the lesser-known Inklings. Peter Kreeft describes it as the most terrifying book he has ever read. Part of the terror comes from Williams's bold exploration of time as a cosmic instrument, like space, for salvation.

Yet Williams's vision is less esoteric than it seems at first glance. C. S. Lewis tackles the same theme in the Narnia books, albeit less confrontationally. When Lucy first enters Narnia through the wardrobe, she spends hours and hours with Mr. Tumnus and returns convinced that her siblings will be out of their minds with worry about her. But it turns out that "hours and hours" in Narnia is no time at all in our world. Time, it seems, is less linear, and less definite, than we think.

What Lewis evokes is the experience we have all had of eternity and time butting up against each other, one existing inside the other, as it were, all around us. "Time is elastic in our personal experience," says Italian physicist Carlo Rovelli.[1] Think about a child at play. He is utterly absorbed in his task of building or stacking or sorting or whatever it is that has captured him, and to his mind, no time is passing at all. In fact, even that is too timely a statement; he has utterly left time. Reentering it can come as a shock, at least for my children. The end of this kind of mystical playtime often comes with tears and frustration; no matter how long it has gone on, no matter what activity we have scheduled next, they feel eternity slipping out of their grasp, or, conversely, they feel time closing in on them, and it breaks their hearts.

We can call these conflicting experiences of time *chronos,* *kairos,* and the much less familiar *aion.* These are named after the three Greek gods of time. Chronos is where we get our word *chronological.* Time is time moving along as moments on a clock, measurable, predictable, relentless. It just keeps marching, and we must march along with it or be left behind. Kairos time, however, is not measurable by clocks and stars. It is *right* time, or *appropriate* time. It is God's time; it is time-in-eternity, if you will, when the meaning of time itself becomes clear.

Think of the gorgeous "there is a time" passage from Ecclesiastes 3, one of the better bits of poetry humanity has ever written:

> A time to be born and a time to die.
> A time to plant, and a time to pluck up
> that which is planted.
> A time to kill, and a time to heal.
> A time to destroy, and a time to build.
> A time to weep, and a time to laugh.
> A time to mourn, and a time to dance.[2]

When the passage was translated from Hebrew to Greek, "time" was always translated as kairos. Kairos is eternity peering in through the windows of this little house we call chronos and beckoning. Finally, *aion*, which gives us "aeon" and "eon," is eternity itself.

The question of what time is has plagued us for millennia. Time, the medium in which we exist, the water of our sea, tortures us. But the very fact of that torture—the fact that our greatest minds have tried to unravel the mystery of time—tells us something interesting about our relationship with time. Water does not torment fish, and birds do not decry the winds for changing in the fall. Yet time, our atmosphere, is our greatest burden, and we pour countless resources—including time itself—into finding ways to control it.

We are immersed in time, and it takes serious imaginative effort to get ourselves "out" of time, as it were, to think about it. Our experience of time is linear; barring those brief moments when we enter so fully into an activity or meditation that we escape it, we experience time as a line that we are traveling down. There are points behind us, and points ahead of us. We cannot move ahead, no matter how much we might want to, and once we have passed a point, we cannot return to it.

This is our *experience* of time, but increasingly, our observations of nature are revealing that time itself does not really work like this. Points in time, on a physical level, do not appear to be linear *or* fixed; rather, they behave more like streams in the wilderness, which flow and shift, than like beads strung along a thread.

THE SHIFTING SCIENCE OF TIME

Carlos Rovelli is a scientist; to be more precise, he is a theoretical physicist, and one of the founders of the loop quantum gravity theory. Rovelli and his fellow theorists are trying to give a coherent account for the baffling observations physicists have made on the quantum (sub-atomic) level. Rovelli acknowledges of loop quantum theory, "Am I certain that this is the correct description of the world? I am not, but it is today the only coherent and complete way I know of to think of the structure of spacetime without neglecting its quantum properties."[3]

In *The Order of Time*, Rovelli brings the scientific questions that plague physicists into conversation with philosophical and literary questions of meaning. Rovelli expounds on such staggering scientific theories as Einstein's idea that "the 'present of the universe' is meaningless"[4]; Rudolf Clausius's notion that time and heat are essentially related, and so time can *only* be measured in relation to heat[5]; and Ludwig Boltzmann's disturbing claim that "the difference between the past and the future refers only to *our own* blurred vision of the world."[6]

Rovelli argues from a scientific perspective that on a physical level (meaning a level that can be studied by physics) each of the characteristics we associate with time—unity of flow, direction of flow, and independence or measurability of flow—is an illusion. In other words, time as a physical aspect of the universe is nothing like our experience of it.

Perhaps the easiest way to think about these different views and experiences of time is by thinking about light. Our experience of light is of a wave or a pool; when it is present, it flows everywhere until it hits an obstacle like a wall. But when we study light on the smallest possible level, it is not always a wave; instead we find particles, tiny flecks of energy that interact with flecks of matter. What we experience when we see "light" is that interaction: particles of white light hitting a brick wall, and certain particles absorbing into the wall while certain other particles bounce off and return to our eyes, communicating the color "brick red" to our corneas.

Time, it seems, may be much more like light than we have previously thought. Rather than being a smoothly flowing line, it seems to be made up of a whole collection of interactions; what we call "time" is merely a description of the results of those interactions. As Rovelli says, time is roughly reducible to change; that is it.

THE FIELDS OF TIME

Recall that this is a scientific view of time; Rovelli is writing about what happens to time at a micro-level. Knowing all this does not fundamentally alter how we live our lives—at least not yet. But it does shift the balance a bit. It forces us to think of time—and differences in time—as existing in much the same way as space. Whereas humans have long thought of time as a linear, fluid thing and space as a multi-dimensional, more or less static thing, it seems that on a very very small level, time and space are much more similar than that: they seem to both be multi-dimensional *and* fluid. Linearity and stability are both illusions of scale.

Now, why does any of this matter? Surely none of us are going to start living as if time wasn't linear; after all, we all know that at one end of our lives, we are born, and at the other end, we die. Everything that happens in between is our life. We cannot move backward or, except at one fixed speed, forward. If this isn't linear, what is?

The linearity of our experience of time is certainly real. Even Christ submitted to the experience of time as a linear progression: He was born, He lived, He died. Then He rose again, of course, but His life and death honored and indwelt the sequence of cause and effect we call "time," which God set into motion at the Creation. But submitting to time as an experience of linear progression is not the same thing as being trapped within a time that is only ever a linear progression. In the second scenario, we have no choice; our environment is crushing us, and there is nothing we can do. In the first, we have the opportunity to recognize the medium of time as a means of grace.

Time is much less of a linear progression than it seems; rather, it is a landscape in which we wander. Just as a mountain does not disappear when we can no longer see it, moments do not disappear once we are no longer living them. The phenomenological difference between time and space is that we all seem to inhabit one moment of time together, whereas we are all in different spaces. But could it be that we only *seem* to share a moment of time, and in reality, time is far less fixed than we think?

THE ROAD TO HEAVEN

St. Catherine of Siena is said to have written that "all the road to heaven is heaven." She meant that to the soul completely fixed on Heaven, everything in this temporal life reveals God's love—the love that is Heaven. But if this is true (if we can, in this life, be in Heaven even occasionally), are we not transcending our usual linear experience of time? Are we not punctuating time, the life lived on earth, with non-time, with supra-time, with eternity?

Here is an example of what I mean. Within the Catholic faith, the moment within the Mass where the priest offers the Eucharist to God *is* eternity. In that moment, the faithful who are present pass outside chronos time into kairos time. We are no longer, in a metaphysical sense, embedded in the passing of moments and hours; instead, we have entered a mode of time in which Jesus, as the Sacrificial Lamb, is pleading constantly, interceding before God for our souls. Catholics do not believe that Christ is again placed upon the Cross at every single Mass; rather we believe that Christ's sacrifice on the Cross occurred both in chronos time *and* in kairos time. It punched through, as it were, the boundary between modes of time, and now all our times are held together by Jesus. The motto of the Carthusian order of monks is *Stat crux dum volvitur orbis*: "The Cross is still, while all the earth is moving." Moving through space, yes, but also through time.

In other words, once time is not a regimented, mechanical thing for us, but a conglomeration of consequential experiences and relations, we can live differently. We need not fear time and its passing; rather, we can see the passing of time as a means of knowing grace, of coming to know God in a unique and dear way.

Rovelli may be a scientist, but he writes like a poet. He addresses this conundrum quite beautifully, weaving scientific terminology and poetry together, saying:

> [The elementary particles] do not exist immersed in space; rather, they themselves form that space. The spatiality of the world consists of the web of their interactions. They do not dwell in time; they interact incessantly with each other, and indeed exist only in terms of these incessant interactions. And this interaction *is* the happening of the world: it *is* the minimum elementary form of time that is neither directional nor linear. […] It is a reciprocal interaction in which quanta manifest themselves in the interaction, in relation to what they interact with.[7]

Here I invite you to return to what we know about God: that God is What Exists Beyond All Else, that God is Three in One, Triune, and that all that exists flows from the interactions between the Three Persons of God. In the beginning God creates, and He speaks within and amongst Himself ("Let *Us* make man in *Our* image"). At the Baptism of Jesus, all Three Persons appear to our senses: Christ the Son, the Dove the Spirit, and the Voice the Father. Baptism, in the mind of the Church, is an act of cleansing and rebirth—an act of creation. All that we have comes to us through the interactions of the Three Persons of God. Second Corinthians 5:17 says, "Therefore, if anyone is in Christ, he is a new creation; the old has gone, the new has come!"

There is a more excellent way than the clinical word "interactions" for talking about the relationships between the Divine Persons: the word "love." Join me in a flight of imagination: let us replace the word "interactions" in Rovelli's passage with this word "love." Listen to this quantum physicist saying that at the lowest level, the level we cannot yet even see but can only observe from a reverent distance:

> [T]here are things that "do not exist immersed in space; rather, they themselves form that space. The spatiality of the world consists of the web of their *love*. They do not dwell in time; they incessantly *love each other*, and indeed exist only in terms of this incessant *love*. And *this love is the happening of the world*: it is the minimum elementary form of time that is neither directional nor linear.

Most astonishingly, he is speaking about "a reciprocal love in which quanta manifest themselves *in love,* in relation to *what they love.*"

Perhaps at this point you've begun to think, *This is crazy,* or worse, *This sounds like mysticism!* In either case, you'd be right. Reality is crazy—crazier and more wonderful by far than we can begin to imagine. Mystical theology is the sane response to the wonder of the created order. And Rovelli, a bona fide scientist, might agree with me. Elsewhere in *The Order of Time,* he writes this poignant passage:

> As human beings, we live by emotions and thoughts. We exchange them when we are in the same place at the same time, talking to each other, looking into each other's eyes, brushing against each other's skin. We are nourished by this network of encounters and exchanges. *But, in reality, we do not need to be in the same place and time to have such exchanges.* Thoughts and emotions that create bonds of attachment between us have no difficulty in crossing seas and decades, sometimes even centuries, tied to thin sheets of paper or dancing between the microchips of a computer (emphasis added).[8]

This is objectively true. By material means like paper or microchips, we routinely overstep space and time to speak to one another. That in itself is marvelous: that we, creatures of dust submerged in time, can transcend time and space constantly and speak to other souls far removed from us in the landscape of space and time.

It leaves a question unanswered, though. Can we, as Christians, create these bonds even *without* paper or computers, but solely through the action of exchange that we call prayer? Can we slip, even erratically and unsustainably, beyond the bounds of time into a mode of existence that is not bound to follow the causal unfolding that we call "time"—a mode we call by the beautiful name "eternity"?

Of course we can. In fact, we must.

ROAMING THE LANDSCAPE OF SALVATION

In his final book *Letters to Malcolm,* C. S. Lewis probes the relationship between prayer and time, and I am not aware of a better summary than his:

> Our prayers are granted, or not, in eternity. Our prayers, and other free acts, are known to us only as we come to the moment of doing them. But they are eternally in the score of the great symphony. Not 'pre-determined'; the syllable *pre* lets in the notion of eternity as simply an older time. For though we cannot experience our life as an endless present, we are eternal in God's eyes; that is, in our deepest reality. When I say we are 'in time' I don't mean that we are, impossibly outside the endless present in which He beholds us as He beholds all else. I mean, our creaturely limitation is that our fundamentally

timeless reality can be experienced by us only in the
mode of succession.[9]

What effect on our day-to-day existence then comes from
being "eternal in God's eyes"? I am no saint. I am no mystic.
I myself have only glimpsed the hills and valleys of the Land
of Salvation through the eyes of others—Williams, Rovelli,
St. Catherine, Lewis, and many more. I myself cannot say that I
roam these hills freely. But from what I have seen, roaming those
hills is far more possible than we may be inclined to believe.

When we think of time in this way, our approach to prayer
is transformed. If time is not merely a straight line which we
ride for a while before falling off, but in its fullness a broad,
dynamic landscape—if time is much more like eternity than we
experience it to be—then we have a great deal more freedom
in how we pray. We need not confine ourselves to praying for
the future; indeed, we can pray for the past—and we can rest
assured that our prayers are heard and granted in eternity,
where God is. For example, suppose that someone we love has
died, and we are not happy with the relationship we had with
that person. If time is much less of a line and more of a landscape, we can truly and faithfully pray *for our past relationship.*
We can beg that God was working in that relationship beyond
what we knew, and we can look forward to experiencing the
answer to those prayers in eternity.

ETERNALLY PRESENT

All this—this vision of time as a landscape rather than a line—also has the power to transform how we live *within* time. The devil has managed to turn time into a double-edged sword, slicing at us with nostalgia or regret over the past and poisoning us with dread or abstract ambitions about the future—and distracting us entirely from the present, our nearest analogy to the experience of eternity. But once we conceive of time as a landscape, the devil loses many of his weapons. We have access to something greater than the tension between living life backwards, facing the past, or forwards, straining into the future. We know that both are safe in eternity. Both will be perfectly redeemed. As T. S. Eliot writes in the *Four Quartets,* "Time present and time past / Are both perhaps present in time future, / And time future contained in time past [. . .] all time is eternally present."

This allows us to truly love. The biggest distractions from love are *past perceived wrongs or losses* and *future abstractions*; we cannot love a person truly if we are fixated either on the past or on the future. Acts of love can only be done in the present. Nowhere is this clearer than in the life of the Lord Jesus: He is always deeply present. Whether with His disciples, His Mother, Pontius Pilate, or the penitent thief on the cross, He is immediately and urgently *with them.* In the few moments where His mind goes to the suffering before Him, there is a clear reason in the present for it; He takes His awareness of the future and, rather than letting it cripple Him, transforms it into a parable or a prayer, which He then gives as a gift. For Jesus, no moment is only chronos; every moment on earth is chronos *and* kairos, perfectly integrated. Every moment, for Jesus, is the right moment.

This, in turn, has the power to allow us to live in faith that every moment of our lives is being saved up for us as an eternal means of grace. "All the road to heaven is heaven." This is what I believe it means to be saved. Salvation is nothing less than a union with God so perfect that we recognize all the moments of our lives as *gifts*—gifts of grace, opportunities to be with God. Lewis puts it this way in *The Great Divorce,* when George MacDonald says to the narrator,

> Not only this valley but all their earthly past will have been Heaven to those who are saved. [They don't know] that Heaven, once attained, will work backwards and turn even that agony into a glory. [The process begins] even before death. The good man's past begins to change so that his forgiving sins and remembered sorrows take on the quality of heaven. [...] And that is why, at the end of all things, when the sun rises here [...], the Blessed will say "We have never lived anywhere except in Heaven."[10]

Adorning Space and Time as God's Image

PETER J. LEITHART

*God is Maker, eternally so. We're made in
His likeness; therefore, we too are makers.
Every human invention is a Little Bang,
a faint reverberation on God's original fiat,
writes theologian Peter Leithart. But how?
And why? And what does this tell us about
our nature, and the promises and
perils of human creativity?*

Niggle, the title character of J. R. R. Tolkien's short story, "Leaf
by Niggle,"[1] is an ordinary, silly man, a modest painter whose
specialty is leaves. He attends to leaves with diligent wonder,
spending "a long time on a single leaf, trying to catch its shape,
and its sheen, and the glistening of dewdrops on its edges." Yet he
aspires to more. Beginning from "a leaf caught by the wind," he
paints a tree. Birds appear, then other trees, then a snow-tipped
mountain in the distance. Soon the painting has grown so large
he needs a ladder to continue the work. He builds a shed to

house the painting, sacrificing a potato patch in the process. The modest leaf-painter has become a titanic world-artist.

Yet Niggle can never bring his painting to a conclusion, in part because his project is "too large and ambitious for his skill." Besides, he's fairly good at other tasks, so he's often enlisted to help his neighbors, especially the lame Mr. Parish. The demands of daily life keep Niggle from his work:

> Things went wrong in his house; he had to go and serve
> on a jury in the town; a distant friend fell ill;
> Mr. Parish was laid up with lumbago; and visitors kept on
> coming.

Parish's wife is feverish; her husband is too lame to go up and down the stairs; the wind has blown tiles off the roof; the excuses mount, and Niggle is called in to help. In his obsession with his painting, Niggle regards these requests for help as interruptions, beneath notice for an elevated tree-painter. Niggle neglects his Parish in his ambition to capture the world.

Tolkien's cautionary tale about the dangers of creative hubris echoes a regular theme of the Christian tradition: whatever human creativity is, it's radically different from God's creativity. This is what Niggle forgets: God alone creates. This truth is a variation of the basic axiom of Christian faith: *God* is God, and you're *not*.

But this crucial truth sometimes leads us to disparage the marvels of the action and creativity of the *imago Dei*. As the church fathers often said (echoing Plato), God is not envious. He isn't stingy with His gifts. Knowing human nature means not only knowing our difference from God, but also our resemblance to Him. To the axiom above, we need to add another: God is God, and you're His *image*.

IMAGE OF GOD

Everything that is, writes Thomas Aquinas, is an effect of the ultimate cause, which is God. Since effects are like their causes, each and every thing, in the inner core of its existence, resembles the Creator who made and loves it. Thomas says there are three degrees of likeness. First, some things are like God simply by existing. Since God is Himself "Being" or *esse*, every existing thing is like God to some degree. Second, living things are even more like the living God; and third, things that know or understand are most like God, who is intellectual substance.[2]

This all might seem a little academic, but it actually has profound ramifications for the way we moderns think about ourselves and our relationship with creation and creating. While all creatures bear some likeness to God, only the last category— rational creatures—have the likeness of an image rather than a likeness of a mere trace.

This last category is us. In us, God's likeness becomes an image. Now, a likeness can become an image only when the likeness in question is a *specific* likeness. A son is an image of his father, because the likeness between father and son is a likeness within a species; a son looks like his father. A king's likeness on a coin is also an image, because the shape on the coin bears a specific likeness to the specific ruler.

The human body bears a *trace* of likeness to God, but in that it's no different from any other created thing. Our intellect, though, has the likeness of an *image*. For Thomas Aquinas, the image of God is found exclusively in the human mind. The resemblance is very precise. It's not simply the similarity between "God thinks" and "man thinks." To Thomas, divine intellect is Triune, and the human mind imitates this Triune pattern:

> [A]s the uncreated Trinity is distinguished by the procession of the Word from the Speaker, and of Love from both of these … so we may say that in rational creatures wherein we find a procession of the word in the intellect, and a procession of the love in the will, there exists an image of the uncreated Trinity, by a certain representation of the species.[3]

As the Father generates a Word and the Father and Son breathe forth the Spirit who is Love, so the human mind forms an inner word (imagination, intelligence, reason, etc.), and the will impels the human mind to love.

This is quite wonderful. But even this is not the whole story. This triadic explanation of the *imago Dei* still doesn't quite capture the emphasis we find in the first chapter of Genesis, where the phrase "image of God" is first used. The Hebrew term for "image" (see Genesis 1:26–27; *tzelem*) is commonly used of idols (see Numbers 33:52; 2 Kings 11:18), which visually represent the authority and presence of a god. The creation account is a temple-building narrative, and as the construction comes to its climax, God sets His image within His cosmic house. In forming man, the Creator represents His presence. By placing man in His world, the Creator asserts His authority. Unlike the images of the dead gods of the nations, the image of the Creator is an embodied, living soul. Adam's materiality and visibility is, in Genesis, essential to his being the image of God.

To be image is to be the visibility of the invisible God.

IMAGE OF THE CREATOR

But God doesn't have a body, so how do human beings visibly manifest the Creator? Genesis 1:26 links the image of God with man's vocation to rule other creatures. Yet to get a full picture of how humans are the image of God, we need to gather clues from the whole creation account. An image of God is *like* God. To figure out what it means to be made in the likeness of God, we should ask, "What is *God* like?"

By the time we get to Genesis 1:26, we know a lot about God. First and foremost, God "creates" (Heb. *bara'*). The verb is used seven times in the first two chapters of Genesis (1:1, 21, 27 [3x]; 2:3, 4). The Creator is a *Maker*. The verb "make" (Heb. *'asah*) is used ten times in Genesis 1, eight times with reference to things God makes: the firmament (Genesis 1:7), the lights of the heavens

(1:16), the beasts of the earth and cattle (1:25), man (1:26, 31). On the Sabbath, God rests from the "work which He had *made*," that is, "from all His work which He had *made*" (2:2). In case we don't get the point, the author adds, "He rested from all His work which God had created and *made*" (2:3).

As Athanasius observed, God's fruitfulness isn't an addition to God's being. He doesn't *become* productive when He creates. It's not as if God were eternally barren and then became fruitful. The Father eternally creates. He generates the Son as His living Art and Image. The Son is not created—Christianity is clear about that—but He is *produced* by the Breath and Power of the Spirit, as the first (and eternal, both past and future) fruit of the Father's eternal creativity. Within the life of the Trinity, there is a fecundity of which His work of creation is a manifestation. God *is* Maker, eternally so. If we're made in His likeness, we too are creators and makers. Made in His image, we're made to make.

Christians sometimes minimize human creativity. "We don't *make* anything," we say. "We just rearrange what's already there." Thomas Aquinas sounds just this note when he says, "to create can be the action of God alone."[4] Thomas uses a stipulated definition of "create": To create is to be the absolute origin of existence. Thomas wants to protect the uniqueness of God's creative work. Even when we factor in the narrowness of his definition, I suspect Thomas would be profoundly *un*impressed with our early twentieth-century obsession with "creatives" and "creativity."

Thomas is essentially right. God says, "Light, please," and there's light where there's never been light before. He says, "Let the waters teem," and they teem. He says, "Let us make man," and man is. Only God creates this way; we can't create from nothing, simply by speaking. We always use pre-existing raw materials, which we receive as gifts from God. We break them down, mold them, and reassemble them. We don't make animals. We tame them, so they provide work and, eventually, food. We don't make trees. We plant them, cut them down, reshape the wood, and turn it into a shelter. We break and chisel God's stones to make blocks and bricks for temples and palaces. Man is not, as Shakespeare's Coriolanus wished to be, "author of himself." Creatures that we are, we aren't even *fully* authors of the things we author.

Yet we shouldn't over-stress the contrast between God's making and ours. After all, God Himself doesn't make everything *ex nihilo. He* makes from pre-existing material too. God makes the formless void (see Genesis 1:2), He speaks light into existence, and He appears to make other things by pure *fiat.* Overall, Genesis 1 shows God shaping and filling the dark, watery earth He creates in Genesis 1:1–2. He spends the first half of the week forming the dark and formless void, giving it light and shape. He spends the second half of the week filling the spaces He forms. But He doesn't fill the world directly. He speaks to earth, and earth springs up with plants. He speaks to the seas, and fish teem. He speaks to the land again, and beast, cattle, and creeping things come to life. Empowered by the creating Word, the world *fills itself.*

We can draw this rather astonishing conclusion: Creation participates in its own creation. God completes creation by giving creation power to complete itself. With infinite humility, the infinite God creates by giving *creatures* power to create.

God gives unique creative powers to human beings. Enlivened by the Breath of God, commissioned by His Word, we are created to be creative. As J. R. R. Tolkien often put it, human beings are subcreators.[5] Despite his reservations about applying "create" to human making, Thomas comes close to the same conclusion.[6] Because human beings are rational, intelligent beings who are images of God's mind, we're capable of a kind of making that surpasses anything found among animals. And our making images the Trinitarian structure of God's mind. Before I build, say, a birdhouse, my mind generates a plan that is then executed in the outside world. That "interior word" serves as an exemplar for the thing I make, a likeness to the interior Word generated by the Father.[7]

I think we must go further, though. Our creating is like God's in more than this simple analogy. There is a commonality in the process that sparks my imagination. Consider: God uses pre-existing materials to create and make. So do we. God forms and fills, and so do we. God makes *new* things, and so do we. Of course, we first *receive* God's gifts, but when we've reassembled them, we've made *entirely* new things, entirely new *categories* of things. A table isn't merely a rearrangement of wood. It's a *table*, a human creation that doesn't exist in nature. It is a created thing God *didn't* create during the six days. When we've learned to spin metals into filaments, and to harness electricity, and to blow glass, we can make a new thing: an electric light.

Every human invention is a Little Bang, a faint reverberation on God's original *fiat*. We're creative *because* God is creative. But more than we realize, we're creative *in the same way* God is creative.

Further, God makes a *world* He doesn't need. He doesn't dwell in temples made by hands. He isn't served by human hands, as if He needed our help. He gives everything life and breath, for in Him we live and move and exist (see Acts 17:24–28). God makes the world out of sheer delight in making, a sheer desire to share His life and glory with creatures. All the way down and all the way in, creation is gratuitous. At the inner core, everything God has made is a gift of grace.

In this, our making has a uniquely Godlike character. Many things we make with tools aren't necessary for survival. Mill stones and ovens are necessary to bake bread, but we don't *need* bread to keep our biological machine sputtering along. We could, like Jesus's disciples, live on what we rub from ears of grain. We don't need the tools of wine-making because we don't *need* wine.

No animal makes like *that,* like that transforming of grain to bread, of grapes to wine. No animal has made even so simple a tool as a screwdriver, and all animal tools have a direct relation to the animal's basic need for food, water, and shelter. Animals don't adorn. Birds build nests for shelter and to store eggs, but there are no schools of ornithological architecture. Beavers don't put solariums on their dams, and no bear decorates his den with wall paintings commemorating his hunting exploits. No animal makes for the sake of making. Animals play, but no animal could invent cricket or basketball. Animals do wondrous things, but, as Samuel Johnson said, no beast is a cook.

On the other hand, human making always verges toward art. Our work aims at glorifying, beautifying, and enhancing creation and human life. Making *per se* isn't unique to the image of God. *God-like* making and gratuitous creativity: *These* are unique to the image of God. To be the image of God is to be an artist. Artifice isn't an add-on to human nature. It *is* our nature.

TALKING ANIMAL

Man is like God, so we've asked, "What is God like?" God creates. He also speaks, and creates by speaking. The New Testament reveals the fuller truth: God doesn't just speak but *is* Word (see John 1:1–3). The speaking God makes man in His own image and likeness, a speaking creature who can talk back to Him in prayer, praise, conversation, argument. The God who is Word makes human beings by His Word in the image of His Word; similarly, we are equipped to make words and sentences and dramas and epic poems, as well as shoes and ships and sealing wax.

In this too, humans are images of God. Before his first day is over, Adam is using language. He doesn't begin with Neanderthal grunts. He doesn't point and gesture. He uses *words*. Adam uses language to take hold of the world and make it his own. His first act of rule is to name the animals (see Genesis 2:19). It is a Godlike act of "calling" things by name (cf. Genesis 1:5, 8, 10). Adam fulfills the creation pattern in miniature, as observer and participant.

God lights, forms, fills, names. So do we. We shape and fill the world and then give names to our creations. In His infinite humility, God receives *our* naming as His own. God names only a handful of things. The rest He leaves to Adam. Whatever Adam calls something, it bears that name, both for Adam *and* for God (see Genesis 2:19; cf. 2:23 with 3:15). What does God call a laptop? There's no mystery. He calls it a *laptop*. What does God call *me*? He honors my parents by calling me "Peter."

By naming, Adam classifies, but he also discovers; he learns there is no animal helper suitable to him. Adam represents created features of animals in verbal form. There's something "elephanty" about the elephant; the "mammoth" is truly mammoth, and what else would you call a creature so strange as a platypus? At base, Adam *creates* names the same way he creates everything else: He makes them up, *ex nihilo*, as it were. His words don't just *mirror* the world; they shape it. God's speech is creative, and so is Adam's. The names Adam creates *make* the world into a human world, made meaningful by human speech. Without Adam's names, the world remains un-verbalized, still formless and void.

The world is meaningful because it's the product of the Word. But we don't merely discover meaning in creation. Meaning is always meaning-*for*-someone. The world has meaning-for-us when we're able to name it. In the image of the divine Word, imitating the meaning-giving of the Creator, we *make* creation meaningful. Like the Creator, we (the image) create a world by speaking.

Made in the image of God's image, we're image-makers, symbolic creatures. We grasp the world through linguistic symbols. When it dawns on Helen Keller that the cool liquid she touches is "water," she doesn't just get a name. She gets the *thing*. The Word delivers the world. Linguistic symbols form a *shared* world. When I tell you, "That is water," the substance becomes water for *both* of us.[8]

Symbols are more than mere signs or indications of reality; they actually lead to other forms of reality. For example, symbols make human society possible. We commune with one another by communing together in symbols. We say "we" because we are creatures of symbols, created in the image of the God who said "Let us." Every society, Augustine says, is knit together by shared signs and sacraments. Because we make and share symbols, we can be more than a pack or a herd. Speaking together, we form one thing, a body. Symbols enable us to share ideas. As symbol-makers, we can con-celebrate the Eucharist. Sharing common symbols, we become a human replica of the divine society of Father, Son, and Spirit.

By use, word and thing become inseparable. I don't think of the word "water" as a label pasted on an anonymous liquid. The liquid *is* water, and we experience it as actually, even *naturally,* "watery." The symbol seems to contain the thing, and the thing seems to embody the symbol—a mutual indwelling that echoes the mutual indwelling of the Father and His Image, the Speaker and the Word He breathes. We inhabit the world we symbolize as our symbols inhabit us. We make ourselves in making our symbols.

HUMBLE CREATOR

With all this talk about creativity and the power of the human word, I'm in danger of tripping into a Christianized Prometheanism, defining everything by human needs and capacities. To keep my balance, I return to Niggle, to see how the ambitions of Tolkien's leaf-painter are properly tempered and disciplined.

After Niggle catches a fatal cold bicycling in the rain, "the Driver" appears to take him to his final destination. Niggle has to leave his painting behind, uncompleted. Yet he finds redemption in purgatorial therapy at the Workhouse. Like the characters in Dante's *Purgatory*, Niggle is forced to perform the disciplined tasks he's neglected. A negligent gardener in life, he spends ages and ages digging. He ignored Mr. Parish's broken roof, so he's put to work with saw and hammer and paintbrush. After a life of frenetic, mostly fruitless activity, he's forced to sit in the dark and think.

These disciplines chasten and focus Niggle's creative ambitions. A creature's creativity, he learns, doesn't rival the creativity of the Creator. In fact, creating out of rivalry, pride, or ambition is precisely the opposite of imaging the Creator's creativity. Niggle

tried to surpass God by envying God; but God is not envious. On
the contrary, the Creator's own creativity is expressed in care,
sacrifice, and humility. Genuine human creativity must show the
same loving attention to the creation as the Creator.[9]

"Leaf by Niggle" is a meditation on the ethics of time. It's
about idleness, the sloth lying behind busyness, the petty
selfishness that drives our time-consuming projects, our nearly
complete inability to use time wisely. It's also a meditation on
time redeemed. On his return from the Workhouse, Niggle is
astonished to find his tree, "finished ... alive, its leaves opening,
its branches growing and bending in the wind." The whole
landscape is there, even parts he merely imagined for an instant,
strokes that never made it to the canvas.

Niggle can only stare in wonder and utter, "It's a gift!" So it is;
so are all our "creations," for we only ever create as a response to
a prior Word, "Let be!"

In "Niggle's world," Niggle is reconciled with Parish. All his
wasted, mismanaged time is restored. He becomes the creator
he aspired to be only after he yields to the patient rhythms of
eternity. In our creativity, as in every other way, we're fully images
of God only in the end, when imagination proves true.

PART 2

We

CREATE

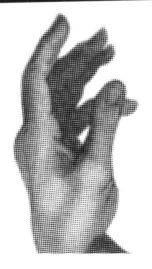

Gratitude: The Foundation of Human Creativity

LESLIE BUSTARD

*Poet and publisher Leslie Bustard's personal
journey through a shadowed valley teaches
us that cultivating attentiveness of what
we've been given—in nature, among people,
through words and the Word—and responding
with gratitude is the key to living lives
of beauty and creativity.*

It is a Sunday evening in January 2020 and I am sitting with my husband and friends at a local restaurant. We're taking in the news that I have melanoma.. My oncologist confirmed that I have stage 2 breast cancer. Now, sitting together at a local restaurant, we process this devastating news. One friend leans close and asks me, "Can you keep looking for beauty in this time? Will you share it with us, this new beauty you find?"

These questions might seem heartless when one is staring at a long death sentence, but to me—and my friend knew this— they were right on the mark. This was the real core of the matter:

how would I, who has continually sought after beauty in my everyday, ordinary life, continue the quest when the road turned into the valley of shadow?

The philosopher Josef Pieper said, "To be conscious of gratitude is to acknowledge a gift."[1] That is a beautiful saying, because it calls us to look at our lives through a lens of gift, to cultivate attention to what we have been given. It does not let us take things for granted.

But there is a dark side to this saying, one that every person in the world has experienced. So often, in our lives in this fallen world, we are given things that we don't want. What are we to do with those things? How can we live with gratitude when our path turns a way we do not want to go?

Walking through that shadowed valley of cancer and seeking after beauty—everywhere from my backyard to my doctor's office—became a journey of discovery for me, a life-lesson of how attentiveness leads to gratitude. This is the means of grace God offered me. He offers this means of grace wherever He calls His children to go.

THE STORY STARTS WITH GIVING

In the beginning and since the beginning, God has woven stories, songs, and poems together, showing us His eternal plans for uniting heaven and earth and humanity to Himself. And lest we be surprised by the outcome, He has also illustrated for us the way our hearts turn and twist and how we follow its desires and loves—sometimes toward Him, but more often in a circuitous, tortuous path away from Him, so that we must be won through tremendous sacrifice.

The Creation Story in the first two chapters of Genesis is our *telos* story. If we pay close attention, we learn for whom and for what we were made—and the key to the story is *gift*. This world, all of it, is God's gift to us. As St. Paul says to the Ephesians,

> Be filled with the Spirit, addressing one another in psalms and hymns and spiritual songs, singing and making melody to the Lord with your heart, *giving thanks always and for everything* to God the Father in the name of our Lord Jesus Christ. (Ephesians 5:18–20 *emphasis added*)

That gives us the key to our identity: we are created and made to live in joyful reception of what God gives.

As Brian Brown reminds us,

> In the beginning was God, Father, Son, and Holy Spirit, a hierarchy of mutual love who was the perfect form of everything good and true and beautiful ... He looked into the disordered nothing, and He spoke meaning—extending His nature to create matter reflecting that nature.[2]

And after all this glorious creation—from heavens to seas to mountains to trees to birds—God created man and woman, to image Him into His world as cultivators, caretakers, and subcreators, doing all in His name and for His glory. God gave the man and the woman a place and a work, and He told them to go out into the world and, in a spirit of gratitude for all He had made, make *more.*

At first, that is what we did. But then we lost our way. Adam and Eve lost sight of creation as God's gift given freely, and instead saw it as something that must be grasped and wrenched. The Tower of Babel account, found later in Genesis, illustrates how Adam's disobedience and sin (as seen in Genesis 3) distorts humanity's motivations and work. Genesis 11:4 says, "... they said, 'Come, let us build ourselves a city, with a tower that reaches to the heavens, so that we may make a name for ourselves; otherwise we will be scattered over the face of the whole earth.'"

Apologist William Edgar writes,

> [H]ere, the city, with its ziggurat [a tower with steps meant to invite God and the gods down to earth] was created for the purpose of making a name for its builders apart from the name of God.... Here the name is an attempt for autonomy.[3]

Sunk in sin, humanity craved autonomy as an "escape" from gifts and the gratitude they merit. The Babel story hearkens back to the story of the Fall, where Adam and Eve rejected gratitude in favor of grasping; taking, rather than receiving what God makes for us.

Obviously, these efforts to escape from gratitude did not work out; the Fall introduced death into the world, and Babel shattered our human community. The story of how God set out to reunite heaven, earth, and humanity to Himself through the life, death, and resurrection of Jesus is woven through the rest of Scripture. As we wait with all of creation for Christ's return, we know we cannot live and create in perfect love like God did at Creation. But we can live and create in a way that rejects being formed by a Tower-of-Babel vision for making.

SLOWING DOWN AND RECEIVING

The first spring and summer of my time in cancer-land were marked by late morning walks and mid-afternoon quiet time, usually sitting outside. My melanoma was initially fought with an infusion of two types of immunotherapy. The side effects of this left me with swollen ankles and knees, and pain in my legs and arms, making it almost impossible to walk or move well. As soon as I was able, after large doses of steroids to reduce the inflammation and pain, I started walking to keep the swelling down. And afterwards, tired out, I would sit on my second-story back porch, looking out into my little corner of the world.

The quiet of this time and the uncertainty of my cancer led me to pay close attention to what was all around me. I determined beauty was going to be my companion and God would be my sustainer, and I sought, in the midst of all the uncertainty and pain, to receive His gifts with open hands.

Blue skies and trails of clouds above me, bird song to the right and to the left of me, and the shadows of branches stretching and playing across the grass in front of me—ordinary life began to shine out in a way I'd never seen before. There were times my daughters had to remind me to pay attention to their conversations because I was easily distracted by the sun stretching down through tree limbs and leaves.

Poems and poets became my friends. I craved words to help me name how raw and vulnerable I felt and the hope I needed in the face of suffering. As I begged for trust in God, no matter what He called me and my family to walk through, I sought to rest in His promise never to leave me or forsake me, and that to keep my eyes on Jesus was a real way to be sustained.

But how to fix one's eyes? How to grow in knowing God's reality in my own mysterious, troubling days? How to cultivate the heart of thankfulness in all things, when "all things" were hard with an unknown end?

The only way I could answer these questions was by trying to pay attention—closer attention than I had ever paid before. God speaks; He speaks through nature, through other people, through the liturgy, through His Word. But so often, we are barely paying attention. For me, these days of pain and darkness became days of quiet, days of depth, where I could truly begin to cultivate the skill of paying attention to all the ways God speaks.

Before I had even read the words of Pieper in *Happiness and Contemplation*, I had begun to learn what he meant when he wrote,

Who among us has not suddenly looked into his child's face, in the midst of the toils and troubles of everyday life, and at that moment "seen" that everything which is good, is loved and lovable, loved by God! Such certainties all mean, at bottom, one and the same thing: that the world is plumb and sound; that everything comes to its appointed goal; that in spite of all appearances, underlying all things is—peace, salvation, gloria; that nothing and no one is lost; that "God holds in his hand the beginning, middle, and end of all that is." Such non-rational, intuitive certainties of the divine base of all that is can be vouchsafed to our gaze even when it is turned toward the most insignificant-looking things, if only it is a gaze inspired by love. That, in the precise sense, is contemplation.[4]

It was in the contemplation of the sustaining love of Jesus that I learned to rest in gratitude.

Flannery O'Connor once prayed to God that He would "please help me push myself aside"[5] so she could know Him better. I stole that prayer from her, and by a miracle of grace in the midst of suffering, God answered it. He allowed me to recognize that wisdom meant receiving His ways and words. It meant allowing Him to make my days be what He deemed right and glorifying.

And then He sent another gift, one I had heard others speak of but could not have believed fully until I experienced it. In this submission and in this resting, my days in cancer-land overflowed with creativity of writing and making that I never would have imagined on my own. I recall especially this poem I wrote during that time, which tries to capture the juxtaposition between my own shifting life and God's constant provision.

The ground is still solid.
Grass is still full of green.
Squirrels still keep running along high wires.
And bees—still searching for clover.
Trees are still playing shadows with the sun.
And the neighbors' flowers, planted last year,
      are blooming white, spilling over their trellis.

Pieper again captured my experience of attentiveness, gratitude, and making when he wrote,

> Out of this kind of contemplation of the created world arise in never-ending wealth all true poetry and all real art, for it is the nature of poetry and art to be paean and praise heard above all the wails of lamentation.... No one can obtain felicity by pursuit. This explains why one of the elements of being happy is the feeling that a debt of gratitude is owed, a debt impossible to pay.... To be conscious of gratitude is to acknowledge a gift.[6]

Daily attentiveness and gratitude became my way of seeking to "cooperate with holy grace in every moment of my existence."[7]

DEEP GRATITUDE

Glory be to God for dappled things—
  For skies of couple-colour as a brinded cow;
    For rose-moles all in stipple upon trout that swim;

Fresh-firecoal chestnut-falls; finches' wings;
  Landscape plotted and pieced—fold, fallow, and plough;
    And áll trádes, their gear and tackle and trim.

All things counter, original, spare, strange;
  Whatever is fickle, freckled (who knows how?)
    With swift, slow; sweet, sour; adazzle, dim;
He fathers-forth whose beauty is past change:
              Praise him.

Gerard Manley Hopkins in his poem "Pied Beauty" shows us
how to pay attention, and then how this attentiveness bears the
fruit of gratitude. His words help us focus on the variety found
in nature, like a multi-colored sky, spotted fish, finches' wings, as
well as how man adds to this variety through how he cultivates
the land. Hopkins is not pointing out beauty that has "clean
lines." He wants us to see the differences and be glad for them, as
well as know the God who saw fit that the earth would be full of
all that is "fickle, freckled . . . swift, slow, sweet."

Living *corem deo*—before the face of God—includes being
attentive to and acknowledging our blessings that go beyond our
imagining. The God whose beauty does not change makes all of
life a gift. His gifts may be found when contemplating a surprise
of swallows swooping low in the early evening, experiencing the
spark of an artistic vision, or receiving the bread and the wine
with one's church community each Sunday. Gratitude flows out
of this living-before-the-face-of-God life.

With the priest-poet Hopkins and other artists, we can learn to enter into the raw grandeur of the world; we learn to use words and images to help others see as well, and then we learn to return the glory to God. When we care how our work affects others, our experiences will show how our attention, imagination, and materials assist our neighbors in beholding and becoming. However, to make for the sake of the world and to the praise of God, we must put aside whatever philosophy pulls us into a Tower-of-Babel mindset. To do this, we need to practice the spiritual discipline of gratitude.

The last line of the first stanza in "Pied Beauty" says "all gear, their tackle, and trim," referring to the tools used by farmers to work with the "plotted and pieced" land. We are reminded that to plough the land or to let it fallow, one must have the right equipment and know-how. So it is with all work that requires experience and expertise to achieve success. Wise artists, those submitting to God's ways of work, will view their materials and tools with gratitude. Tools, even simple ones like a well-sharpened Blackwing pencil, are gifts. Wisdom calls us to hone them to fit our hands and minds well.

In the movie *Babette's Feast*, based on a short story by Isak Dennison, Babette, an acclaimed Parisian cook living as an émigré in a small seaside Jutland village, is an example of what can occur when an artist knows her craft well and then lives into life as one of gift giving and receiving.

Arriving sick and worn out at the doorsteps of a small home, Babette is taken in by two sisters who live there. They lead an old religious community left to them by their father. This community is rife with small and large unresolved grievances. Babette serves these two sisters, and their home and community life are blessed by this care. Later, when Babette wins the lottery, she decides to prepare a magnificent feast for her people. Here the sisters, and the readers, learn the great depths of Babette's talents. Babette knows how to pick the perfect wines and prepare delicious foods—foods her friends had never experienced due to their spartan life.

The sisters are fascinated by a turtle that Babette purchases, yet taken aback that it will be put into a soup. Later at the feast, they taste the soup and realize they have never eaten anything as exquisite as this. Each aspect of the feast softens her guests' hearts to the goodness of the food and forgiveness toward each other. Babette the artist, out of gratitude and love for this small religious community and desiring to use her talents and her tools, creates a meal that brings wholeness to her people.

When we place ourselves at the center of our ambitions, it becomes easy to compare our gifts with others', "to desire this man's art and that man's scope, with what I enjoy contented least" (Shakespeare *Sonnet 29*). But living rightly before God calls us to take gratefully the materials we have been given—imagination, paints, cameras, pencils, vocal cords—and learn to use them with excellence, for others.

Artist Ted Prescott says of the inspiration and the work,

I am often grateful for the "idea," the inspiration. But then comes the hard task of finding the form, the pursuit of which can literally take years. The initial gratitude is long gone, and it's only when the necessary form is found that gratitude returns. Then all that wrestling and the dead ends are seen as necessary and good.[8]

But what of these "wails of lamentation"? How do we "cooperate with holy grace"[9] and live a life of attentiveness and gratitude when our road goes through valleys darkly shadowed? Or when the work goes too long after the inspiration? Our days are filled with joy, love, and creativity, but also with sorrow, brokenness, fear, and anxiety. In the midst of horror and death, how do we even attempt to "[give] thanks always and for every-thing to God the Father in the name of our Lord Jesus Christ . . ."?

TEACH US TO NUMBER OUR DAYS

Since the day my doctor confirmed I had stage 2 breast cancer *and* stage 4 melanoma, the psalmist's words have been shaping my prayers: "Teach us to number our days so that we can gain a heart of wisdom."

In November 2021, close to the two-year mark of living with cancer, I had been tumor-free for six months. I found myself ready to know a specific detail about the BRAF inhibitors that had been keeping the melanoma from spreading again. These meds are powerful and fast-acting, but not proven to be durable. I asked my oncologist how long they are known to work. According to different studies, he said, patients have lasted two to five years on these particular meds. Although the doctor assured me that we would try other treatments when the BRAF inhibitors stopped working, my understanding of the shadowed mystery of my life was brought into sharp focus.

That Christmas season, God showed me how Mary, the mother of Jesus, could be a guide for how to live the days given to me. Her faith in God and her submission to His plan showed me how to pray for these things for myself.

Luke 1 and 2 hint that Mary knew that difficulty and death faced her in the wake of the angel's message. Gabriel, the angelic messenger, revealed that God's plan was for her to bear God's Son, a message Mary received with faith and humility. After this, despite being pregnant, unwed, and facing a long road of hardship, she visited her cousin Elizabeth, where she bore witness to God's grace through a song of gratitude and praise.

> My soul magnifies the Lord,
> and my spirit rejoices in God my Savior,
> for he has looked on the humble estate of his servant.
> For behold, from now on all generations will call me blessed;
> For he who is mighty has done great things for me,
>   and holy is his name. (Luke 1:46–49)

After giving birth to Jesus, and in accordance with God's law, she and Joseph took the infant to the temple and offered their sacrifices. Simeon, a prophet, greeted them, and taking Jesus in his arms, gave thanks that God had fulfilled the promise that Simeon would not die until he saw the Christ. But it is Simeon's words to Mary—that a sword would pierce her soul—that touched my heart. Only God knew when this sword would pierce her heart, just as only He knows when my cancer will no longer be held back by any treatment. Like Mary, I crave the sustaining grace found in her son Jesus. Here is a poem where I reflect on Mary and what she was experiencing.

After Rembrandt's *Simeon and Anna in the Temple*

". . . and a sword shall pierce through your soul." Luke 2:35

Maybe Mary missed those shocking details
Simeon spoke as she looked at Jesus in
his ancient arms. With her memories of
angels and shepherds, one could understand
any weariness at unexpected
words. Except, she was in the habit of
listening to astonishing and strange
prophecies—as if she knew the ways of
the world were revealed through donkeys and old
men. (I think I would have asked one or two
questions and maybe for a timeline.) Yet
young Mary had been learning that even
as a small candle breaks the shadowed dark,
hard paths are lightened by sustaining grace.[10]

Jesus, the Son of God, is the light on our hard paths and the good shepherd in our dark valleys. He is the teacher who guides us into a life of obedience and gratitude. Jesus is trustworthy— although He knew He was walking to His death on a cross, He still loved people, performed miracles, taught about God's kingdom, celebrated weddings and festival days, and worshiped the Father.

Just like Jesus, weeping in the garden and begging the cup of death to be passed by Him yet still submitting to the Father's ways, we submit to how God plans our days even if they are filled with sorrow. And we know that in the death, resurrection, and ascension of Jesus, our life is hidden in His, and we have more than we know for which to be grateful.

When we learn to root ourselves deeply in the soil of gratitude and when we speak words of thanksgiving and sing psalms to each other, we proclaim true wisdom to all in the heavens and on the earth: "God is God and he is not mocked. This is God's world . . . Thanksgiving to God in the name of Jesus Christ announces that death and sin and sorrow have been defeated and Christ is making all things new."[11]

Praise Him.

The Art of Memory

HEIDI WHITE

Humanity's two ways of knowing—the rational
(logos) *and the imaginative* (mythos)—*have
since antiquity been intertwined, says classicist
Heidi White. Culture-making art, music, and
storytelling have been the primary way we tell
ourselves who we are. Yet modernity, and at
times the modern Church, has sundered* logos
and mythos, *elevating what we mistakenly
think is "rational." How are we to respond
to this diabolical dichotomy?*

For me, reason is the natural organ of truth, but
imagination is the organ of meaning. — C. S. Lewis[1]

The oldest Greek mythologies tell the story of all-powerful Zeus,
the father of gods and men, and his lover, Mnemosyne, the
goddess of memory and language. Zeus visits Mnemosyne for
nine consecutive nights, and she gives birth to nine daughters
called the Muses who become the goddesses of art and learning.
The Muses invent music, astronomy, philosophy, geometry,

grammar, rhetoric, poetry, painting, sculpture, theater, architecture, drawing, and dance. Delighted by their creations, the Muses in turn inspire worthy humans to imitate them, thereby forging a fruitful bond between divine and human creativity. The analogy, of course, is rather straightforward: the union of God and memory begets creativity.

Memory has always been the fundamental ground-of-being of art and culture. What we remember makes us who we are. We create artifacts in order to memorialize, to preserve, to remember. Even destructive or revolutionary art is based on memory insofar as it revolts against it, reminding us that our personal and public memories often hold immense cruelty, injustice, suffering, and distortion. Memory is at once individual, communal, and spiritual. And on all three levels, memory endures mainly in images and narratives; indeed, memory nearly always enshrines itself in myth.

In his masterful treatise on Christian classical education titled *Norms and Nobility*,[2] David Hicks distinguishes between two fundamental kinds of knowledge: *logos* and *mythos,* which roughly correspond to reason and imagination. According to Hicks, "the *mythos* represents man's imaginative and, ultimately, spiritual effort to make this world intelligible; the *logos* sets forth his rational attempt to do the same." *Mythos*, then, is the basis of imaginative work—art, music, literature, poetry, dance, and the like. *Logos* is the basis of rational work—philosophy, mathematics, engineering, theology, the sciences, and other disciplines that apply human reason.

MYTHOS AND LOGOS IN UNION

These two ways of knowing belong together as intertwining threads, but modernity wants to rip them asunder. The drab epistemology of the modern wasteland insists that *logos* is true and *mythos* is false, useful only as entertainment, propaganda, or syllabi. In response, dissident subcultures such as New Age religions and popular pseudo-psychologies elevate *mythos* to bizarre heights.

Christians are not exempt from modernity's denuding of knowledge. Instead, Western Christians are often conditioned from within the Church to understand faith as *logos* but not *mythos*. Others reject the propositional *logos* of the faith to interpret the Christian story as mere mythology. Thus *mythos* and *logos* are pitted against each other, and we are put in the position of choosing a side.

But this division is an utterly false and diabolical dichotomy. Christianity is at once rational and mystical, true and beautiful, intellectual and imaginative. Through Christ, the historic Christian faith is the nexus and the union of imaginative *mythos* and rational *logos*. The renaissance of the Christian imagination is reclaiming the vital, essential role of *mythos* in human formation. This does not mean that the faith is a myth in the sense that it is a lie or a metaphor; rather, Christianity is *mythos* in the sense that it is a meaning-making story that ennobles and forms the soul. Hicks speaks to the power of such stories: "A good myth, like a good map, enables the wanderer to survive, perhaps even to flourish, in the wilderness."[3]

Although Hicks writes specifically about education in his treatise, his words apply beyond their immediate context. Indeed, Hicks argues for a vision of education that instills the entire *mythos* and *logos* of culture. He invites us to the pursuit of a Christian *paideia*—a concept deeply appropriate to Christian creative efforts because *paideia* is the Greek word for both education and culture.

PAIDEIA: A UNIFIED VISION FOR LIFE

To the Greeks, there was no distinction between the education of an individual and the cultivation of the culture that forms the communal life of that individual. A person is a microcosm dwelling within rings of three concentric circles (Self, Society, and the Universal). Each individual Self exists in the smallest, innermost ring, surrounded and enclosed by a larger ring that is a communal Society with its normative way of life, surrounded still further out by the Universal circle that is the realm of eternal transcendence, or the "permanent things" as G. K, Chesterton called them. These permanent things are eternal realities like holiness, goodness, truth, beauty, love, justice, wisdom, and the like. To the ancient mind, *paideia* was the whole package; all three circles passed intact from one generation to the next.

In *The Republic*, Socrates argues that the city is like the soul.

Both proceed from pre-existing Forms, and therefore we ought to rule our souls and our cities by the standard of the Eternal Good. Socrates's unified vision for the virtuous life articulates the basis of ancient *paideia*. *Paideia* offers a meaningful, unified, normative being-in-the-world; it instills how to live individually, communally, and spiritually.

Unlike the pagan version, however, Christian *paideia* has the benefit of truth and completion through Christ. Socrates casts an idealistic vision, a shadow, but Christ is the source and the fulfillment of all *logos* and *mythos*. Developing and preserving a Christian *paideia* is the beating heart of any meaningful renewal of Christian imagination. Hicks writes that it is "for the world's fight and the soul's salvation," and this twofold mission is the *telos*—the purpose, goal, ultimate end—of Christian creative effort.

Some may find the appeal for a Christian *paideia* over-whelming or unattainable, but thankfully, we do not have to start from scratch. A rich and vast Christian *paideia* already exists in the Church, the natural world, and the Great Tradition of art, literature, knowledge, exploration, and discovery. All truth and error throughout time and space stand or fall in relation to God and therefore are included or disputed within the universal *paideia* that is the shared *logos* and *mythos* of creation from Eden until this very moment. Thus, we cultivate and preserve Christian *paideia* neither to reconstruct nor to overthrow, but to remember. We are not culture warriors but culture keepers. Christians are the true guardians of the collective memory of the world.

THE MEANING-MAKING OF MYTH

With this in mind, it becomes clear that personal and public narratives serve a fundamentally meaning-making function. Our identities are intrinsically tied to the stories we tell ourselves. To the private individual, this is the realm of psychology and spirituality. But in the public square, it is a matter of myth. Myths are stories that shape entire cultures. They are the basis of all *paideia*, embedded within us as the furniture of our minds. We become what we behold—George Washington confessing he chopped down the cherry tree, Daniel sleeping safely in the Lion's Den, Prometheus chained to the rock, Helen Keller thrusting her hands under the water pump, Icarus plummeting from the sky, Christ suffering on the Cross. Some of these stories are fiction, some fact, but all are myths.

Myths express eternal truths in simple narratives and images, holding enormous normative power for individuals and cultures. The meaning-making function of myth can be seen in these very pages—the story of the birth of the Muses invites both simple acceptance and endless contemplation. Reams of learned pages could not plumb the depth and span the breadth of such a story. And that is only one myth, the telling of which is contained in one sense in a few sentences and in another the whole world. Myth has the power to take us beyond ourselves, beyond our world, into the realm of transcendence.

Myth both invites and defies interpretation and judgment. Because myth makes meaning, it entwines with the rational way of knowing, *logos*, with its inherent urge to interpret, to rightly define, quantify, compare, and understand. Myth's meaning-making faculty also unites with *logos* to make judgments that lead to action. But *logos* is more influenced by *mythos* that we recognize. For example, a materialist *paideia* that elevates technological progress will treat a forest very differently than a pagan *paideia* that believes in tree spirits dwelling within roots and branches. According to the one, trees are natural resources to be exploited; to the other they are sacred vessels to be protected. Both interpretations and their resulting actions are based not merely on self-conscious *logos* but on underlying, often subconscious *mythos.* This aspect of *mythos* defies logical interpretation and rational judgment; in fact, it determines what we think of as "rational." We simply do not recognize how profoundly story-formed we are.

This is not to say that *mythos* is subjective. The modern mind wants to label *logos* objective and *mythos* subjective. But this is a mistake. Logical reasoning can lead to erroneous conclusions just as inherited mythology can lead to flawed beliefs. The problem is not that people put their faith in myths, but that they put faith in the wrong myth. C. S. Lewis recognized this. The story of Christ, he wrote, is simply a true myth; a myth working on us the same way as the others, "but with this tremendous difference—that it really happened." The solution to the problem of *mythos* is not to reject myths but to recover and redeem false myths with the Christian story. Christians are both the story-keepers and the storytellers of the true myth.

PRINCIPLES FOR A
CHRISTIAN PAIDEIA

All of this raises vital questions about content. What should be included in our Christian *paideia*? What do we do about false and wicked *mythos* and *logos*? How do we decide what to preserve and what to create? These vital questions bring us back to the importance of memory. The true myth is very old and much has been built upon it, so it behooves us to follow the following essential guiding principles in contemplating the development and preservation of Christian *paideia.*

First and foremost, Christian *paideia* is founded on the true myth, which is the life of Christ. The gospel is the union of rational *logos* and imaginative *mythos,* the loveliest and truest story ever told. Everything that came before led to it, and everything that happened since proceeded from it. Therefore, the proper place for building and keeping Christian *paideia* is the Church, which St. Paul called "the pillar and ground of the truth." Christians who are faithful participants in the communal life of the Church are nourished by word and sacrament, which are the united *logos* and *mythos* of the faith. Simply keeping the traditions of the Church is a radical act of culture-keeping in the contemporary wasteland.

Secondly, for Christians, all is Christ's, not only within the Church, but even outside it. Christian *paideia* gathers all knowledge and culture under Christ's authority. The misguided *mythos* of modernity elevates an imagined future above the actual past, but

Christians must resist the temptation to forget the past because through Christ all things belong to us. This is not to say that every artifact of cultural memory is good or true. *Mythos* may hold the collected memory of the world, but more often than not the world got it wrong. Through Christ, however, we fill in the gaps.

In his masterful sermon on Mars Hill in the book of Acts, St. Paul declares that the Athenian shrine "to an unknown God" opens up a cultural space for Christ to fill. Rather than degrading the surrounding pagan culture, Paul reclaims it as a Christian inheritance, "that they should seek the Lord, if haply they might feel after him, and find him, though he be not far from every one of us; for in him we live and move, and have our being; as certain also of your own poets have said" (Acts 17:27–28 KJV).

The idolatrous shrine and the platonic poets are aspects of a false pagan *mythos* whose meaning St. Paul redeems through revelation, illuminating and transfiguring the vacant and flawed elements in the light of Christ. The true myth reconciles the false myth. Later, St. Paul proclaims that "all things are yours, whether Paul, or Apollos, or Cephas, or the world, or life, or death, or things present, or things to come; all are yours, and ye are Christ's, and Christ is God's" (1 Corinthians 3:21–23 KJV).

Christ reconciles all things to Himself—including the world's cultural and intellectual heritage. The renaissance of the Christian imagination is a recovery effort and a creative one. We need Christian scholars, storytellers, readers, writers, educators, bards, curators, and enthusiasts. In fact, Christians ought to be the most exuberantly curious and intellectually hospitable people on the face of the earth because all things are ours.

Thirdly, Christian *paideia* is an unfolding story, not a closed canon. We need Christian creators in this generation—writers, poets, musicians, singers, dancers, painters, craftsmen, and more. "Indeed," wrote Tolkien, "only by myth-making, only by becoming 'sub-creators' and inventing stories, can Man aspire to the state of perfection that he knew before the Fall."[4] Christians should be the most zealous and skilled artists in the world. But we do not hold to an empty belief in "art for art's sake," nor do we create to express ourselves, save the world, accumulate glory, or win culture wars. Such creative ethics are foreign to us. Instead, Christians create to remember.

WHAT TO DO WHILE
WAITING FOR THE LORD

The ancient myth of Odysseus tells of the hero's exile and home-coming. During his long years of perilous journeying, Odysseus's wife, Penelope, yearns for him. She raises her son, Telemachus, without his father. Meanwhile, debauched suitors vie for her hand, but she scorns them. To keep them at bay, wise Penelope announces that she cannot marry again until she weaves a burial shroud for her father-in-law, Laertes. Every day for three years, clever Penelope weaves the shroud by day and unravels it by night, buying time for her husband and lord to return.

Like Penelope, we are the King's beloved, stranded in our own homeland, surrounded by dangers and temptations, yearning for the return of the King. The waiting is a Christian dilemma in every generation, which raises the question: while we wait for our Lord to return, what shall we do? We can imitate Penelope, who hatched a daring plan. She knew she could not save herself, but she could take action in the waiting. And what was that action? Penelope *created something*. She oriented her skill to crafting an artifact (the shroud) that remembered the generation before her (Laertes) in order to preserve the one presently in her keeping (Telemachus). The shroud embodies far more than Penelope's quiet wisdom. It reveals the creative vocation.

This is why we strive for a Christian *paideia*. Like Odysseus, our Lord is coming home, and when He does, He will slaughter the suitors, reclaim the land, and restore His bride to her rightful place beside Him. He will wipe the tears from her eyes and crown her with glory for her faithfulness. Indeed, long after Penelope's shroud devolved into a heap of tangled string, the poets sang of prudent Penelope. The following tribute to Penelope is from the ghost of Agamemnon, whose own wife betrayed and murdered him.

Oh fortunate son of Laertes, Odysseus of the many devices, surely you won yourself a wife endowed with great virtue. How good was proved the heart of blameless Penelope, Ikarios' daughter, and how well she remembered Odysseus, her wedded husband. Thereby the fame of her virtue shall never die away, but the immortals will make for the people of earth a thing of grace in the song for prudent Penelope.

Some scholars claim that the "thing of grace"—the "song for prudent Penelope"—is *The Odyssey* itself. If that is the case, we do well to imitate her wisdom.

And what is that wisdom? She remembered her husband. Her great love for her absent bridegroom overflowed in offerings to the waiting. Every generation needs its Penelopes: the artists, poets, songwriters, and craftsmen who will weave and unravel artifacts that tell the true myth over and over again. Like Penelope, may we be prudent and faithful, and may it be said of us, "how well she remembered her wedded husband."

The Art of Cultivation

GRACE OLMSTEAD

*God calls on all humanity to participate
in His work of cultivating His creation.
Yet, as writer Grace Olmstead reminds us,
we have not loved it enough. We are surrounded
by God's beauty and bounty, but we struggle
to comprehend a category between destruction
and preservation. How can Christians embrace
the Creation Mandate and be active
participants in cultivating the created order?*

Every spring at our old farmhouse in Virginia, a pair of finches would nest in the hanging plant I placed on our porch. As soon as I hung it outside in April, they took over: rummaging about to find the perfect spot for their eggs, nibbling off strands of petunia vine, adding bits of found objects from the garden and yard to their creation. As I watered the plant through the spring, the finch parents would watch me warily from a nearby tree branch. I peeked inside their nest, careful not to dampen it, and saw their fragile eggs inside. Eventually, I would see hatched baby birds nestled together, sleepy-eyed.

Together, year after year, these finches and I sought to provide a safe spot for these baby birds to grow and hatch. Our shared spring rhythm was oriented around patterns of nesting and nest-protecting that sought to nurture life—a rhythm, I would argue, embedded in the Creation story itself.

In the second verse of Genesis, we read of the "Spirit of God hovering over the face of the waters." The verb *merahefet* in this sentence, often translated as "hover," can also mean "brooded," referring to a mother bird brooding over her young (as it does in Deuteronomy 32:11). What mysterious gentleness exists, then, in God's acts of creation. The act of bringing order from chaos emerges as a powerful work of the Holy Spirit—one forged in the immense tenderness we associate with a bird that is "nesting." In the fragility of life, in its tenuousness, God is present: and the cultivation of life happens in and through love's enclosing of this fragility.

In pondering the Creation Mandate in Genesis—God's call on humanity to steward the earth—this essay considers what it means for humans to participate in God's work of cultivation. The word "cultivate" comes from the Latin *cultiva*, which refers to the tilling of land, and *colere*, "to till; to inhabit; to frequent, practice, respect; tend, guard."[1] As the various meanings of *colere* indicate, the term "cultivation" encompasses something more than tilling and planting: it suggests habits of constancy, care, and stewardship. We can only forge these habits, I argue, in and through the creative, life-nurturing love of God: love embodied in tactile objects and life forms, and in care for these objects and life forms. We are all called to "nest" in this world.

Alas, this is a work we have often done poorly or not at all throughout human history. Humans have often interpreted the commands in Genesis 1:28 to "subdue" and to "have dominion" according to our interests and greed. In a framing of the Creation Mandate that justifies exploitation of God's creatures and earth, humans position themselves not in harmony with, but in opposition to, plant and animal life on the earth. In our efforts to bring "order" to wild places, we destroy as much or more than we create. In our agricultural efforts to subdue the soil, we denude it and spray it with chemicals. And in our creative efforts—from the creation of smartphones to the cultivation of plastics—we create disastrous amounts of waste. We live not in harmony with our ecosystems, but at war with them.

In Fyodor Dostoevsky's novel *The Brothers Karamazov*, a character named Father Zossima tells the story of his brother Markel, who died as a teenager. As he became ill, Markel experienced a remarkable conversion to Christianity. Some of his last words, related by Father Zossima, are captured thus—again drawing our eyes to birds in a garden:

> The windows of his room looked out into the garden, and our garden was a shady one, with old trees in it which were coming into bud. The first birds of spring were flitting in the branches, chirruping and singing at the windows. And looking at them and admiring them, he began suddenly begging their forgiveness too: "Birds of

heaven, happy birds, forgive me, for I have sinned against
you too." None of us could understand that at the time,
but he shed tears of joy. "Yes," he said, "there was such a
glory of God all about me: birds, trees, meadows, sky; only
I lived in shame and dishonored it all and did not notice
the beauty and glory."

"You take too many sins on yourself," Mother used to
say, weeping.

"Mother, darling, it's for joy, not for grief I am crying.
Though I can't explain it to you, I like to humble myself
before them, for I don't know how to love them enough."[2]

Markel here defines sin—not just against our fellow humans,
but against the world itself—in a way few others have managed
to elucidate. We are surrounded by God's glory, and amid that
glory, we have not loved enough. Psalm 104 speaks of God's active
nurturing of the earth—He touches the earth (verse 32), waters
the mountains (13), renews the ground (30), feeds His creatures
(28), and takes away their breath (29). We, in contrast, have been
sleepwalkers, dulled to the vibrant life of the world God has
made. Because of our lack of care, we transgress against God, the
humans made in His image, and the creatures He has wrought
in love.

But Markel also offers a definition of love that speaks to the
rhythms of cultivation this chapter is meant to highlight. He
suggests slightly earlier in this passage that we must "glorify
life" in our work, play, lament, and care for the world. The
right ordering of our work of cultivation must be forged in and

through Markel's joyful grief and attentive humility, through the process of realizing how much more we must love. The Creation Mandate emerges as "the creative effort to contribute to a flourishing world," as Norman Wirzba writes in *This Sacred Life*—an effort in which we tenderly care for human and nonhuman life.[3]

This is, in a sense, starting at the end: with an acknowledgment of our brokenness, of our failure to cultivate and to love God's creation as we ought. It's important, therefore, to now turn back to the beginning: to consider how God displays *colere* in the mythic rhythms of the Creation account, and how the Creation Mandate is both more exciting and more challenging than we often realize.

· · ·

In Genesis 1:28, God tells Adam and Eve,

> Be fruitful and multiply and fill the earth and subdue it, and have dominion over the fish of the sea and over the birds of the heavens and over every living thing that moves on the earth.[4]

The first aspect of this command, in its focus on a proliferation of life, emphasizes our role as subcreators. Our lives should be full of life: in the bearing and tending of children, in our service to the Church, and in the fostering of vibrant communities. To be "fruitful" is to participate in patterns of creation and caregiving God has fostered all throughout His world.

This will mean, for many Christians, having babies and raising children. For others, it will include mentorship and caregiving roles amid singleness or childlessness. For each of us, it involves habits of care for the earth: cultivating practices that fill our communities and ecosystems with life and health, embodying the virtues and truths we hold dear.

It also involves creating things that mirror God's artistry. In Psalm 104, which I quoted earlier in this chapter, our capacity for creativity in response to God's blessing and provision is referenced in verses 14 and 15:

> You cause the grass to grow for the livestock and plants
> for man to cultivate, that he may bring forth food from the
> earth, and wine to gladden the heart of man, oil to make
> his face shine and bread to strengthen man's heart.

Here, God provides for human and nonhuman life alongside each other, but whereas the nourishment of cattle is primary and unmediated, our nourishment has intrinsic creative and artistic implications. We do not just tend plants from the ground—we also, by the grace of God, can transform and order them in creative ways: in, for instance, wine, oil, and bread. All these examples highlight the diverse, multitudinous, and relational *colere* work we are called to as image-bearers.

The verbs "subdue" and "dominion" in the Creation Mandate have troubled many writers and thinkers, however, as they seem to justify the violence and destruction we see in the age of the Anthropocene (in which humans have begun to significantly impact their environment). This emphasizes the importance of reading Genesis 1:28 with an understanding of the Spirit's work of *merahefet*. As we are made in the image of God, our works of creation and cultivation are meant to mirror His own. The Creation Mandate, therefore, must point *toward* the gentleness and tenderness of God's creative work, not away from it. The Hebrew word translated as "subdue" here, *kabash*, implies an ordering and replenishing without violence or cruelty. It suggests instead a gentle work, one that echoes God's own nurturing rhythms throughout Genesis 1. It affirms humanity's active participation in God's work of nesting and enfolding, protecting and cherishing. We, too, can brood in this earth: nurturing it, loving it, ordering it, and seeking its good.

In considering Genesis's patterns of cultivation and creation, it is important to note that things are not just ordered—they are ordered *in relation to each other.* God creates ecosystems: webworks of life that illustrate His own relational nature as a triune God. We as humans are not called to autonomy and isolation, but to live within relationships. Things on earth "live and move and have their being" in Christ—and, in mirroring the Trinity, in and through interdependence.[5] Everything is ordered in love and relationality. Creation's biological arrangement thus conveys the heart of the Gospel, the Trinitarian love at the center of all things. This love connects us to our fellow humans (we are our brothers' keepers), and it connects us to the nonhuman life around us.

This sort of ecosystem-focused cultivation is exemplified in the Year of Jubilee and practice of *shmita* explicated in Leviticus 25.

God commanded the Israelites to let the land lie fallow every seventh year (this was also a time in which slaves would be freed and debts would be cancelled). During this fallow period, the soil could repair itself. Perennial plants could grow. Wildlife could receive needed shelter and sustenance. Even groundwater could be impacted by deep-rooted systems encouraged through the practice.

Shmita suggests to us the grace and love inherent in the Creation Mandate, as humans are called not to consume but to steward God's creatures and plant life. Here, to "subdue" is not to endlessly control, domineer, or oppress God's earth. Rather, it is to seek the harmony and flourishing of the land, its *shalom*. Neither is it about cultivating more profit in ensuing seasons (like many modern sustainability techniques): in an interview, farmer Lucy Zigward suggested that "what sets Shmita apart from typical crop rotations is that it invites us to re-imagine our fundamental relationship with the land. . . . Shmita is a full-stop, reset, rethink of cultivation."[6] Like the practice of leaving food in field corners for the needy, the Year of Jubilee suggests that human rulership of the earth can only be realized in habits of love and care.

In examples such as these, a subduing work is forged in rhythms of humility, in an acknowledgment of the intricate complexity inherent in God's created order. The rhythms of the ecosystems God created are poetic, interlinking and overlapping, creating a web or "meshwork" of life, as anthropologist Tim Ingold puts it.[7] To be proper cultivators of the earth, therefore, requires our patient attention and our wonder. The intricacy and depth of God's creations defy scientific explanation or human mastery.

This is something mothers and fathers often realize with time: no matter how many months we spend caring for our children, and no matter how many children we have, each day of parenting surprises us. To care for God's unique created beings requires constant trust that He will show us how we should cherish them. We obey the Creation/Culture Mandate not through hubris but through a humble awareness of our insufficiency. As Wendell Berry writes in "A Native Hill,"

> We must change our lives, so that it will be possible to live by the contrary assumption that what is good for the world will be good for us. And that requires that we make the effort to know the world and to learn what is good for it. We must learn to cooperate in its processes, and to yield to its limits. But even more important, we must learn to acknowledge that the creation is full of mystery; we will never entirely understand it. We must abandon arrogance and stand in awe. We must recover the sense of the majesty of creation, and the ability to be worshipful in its presence. For I do not doubt that it is only on the condition of humility and reverence before the world that our species will be able to remain in it.[8]

As we attend to the world around us in a spirit of humility, we will see, like Markel, that we have not loved enough. This realization prompts lament as well as reverence. But I would posit that the more time we spend in embodied acts of creation and care—gardening, raising children, building furniture, baking bread, or caring for animals, for instance—the more we are prompted to praise, reciting God's words of benediction and love in Genesis 1, declaring the goodness of this world and of its Creator.

We all yearn, I think, to live life in harmony with nature, no longer striving against thorns. It is what we were made for, after all. In Christ, we see the patterns of stewardship, ordering, and care that draw the whole earth to *shalom*.

As a carpenter, Jesus Himself would have engaged in artistic acts of subcreation: shaping wood into both beautiful and useful objects for human flourishing. In turning water into wine, multiplying loaves and fishes, and calming storms, He demonstrates His power over all creation, and He exercises this power in a way that blesses and nurtures life. In His Sermon on the Mount, He emphasizes God's care for the birds and the lilies, adding that we are of "much more value than the birds."[9] In Jesus's tender attention to little children, widows, and the sick, He patterns the *colere* work we must replicate. The earth flourishes through His presence, His touch. In the life of Christ, we finally see what it would look like to notice God's beauty and glory in His creation, and to "love enough." The Gospels draw our voices to sing and our hearts to delight.

· · ·

We live in a world broken by the Fall. Because of this, we don't always know how to cultivate fruitfulness, or how to reckon with the evil and brokenness around us. How do we respond to pestilence and famine, injustice and violence?

J. R. R. Tolkien's character Tom Bombadil, from *The Lord of the Rings*, is inspiring in this regard—not because he offers solutions to our specific problems, but because he exemplifies a specific way of being. He overflows with song and poetry, and his life is centered around works of cultivation and creation: whether in preparing food and drink for his guests ("yellow cream, honeycomb, and white bread and butter"), carrying home waterlilies for his beloved Goldberry, or in tending to his forest home.[10]

But Tom also shows us how to reckon with fallenness and darkness. He does not fight off evil with viciousness or pride but with persistent and joyful efforts to "tune" the world to its proper key. When Frodo cries out for help in the Old Forest, Tom comes to his rescue. He tells Frodo that he "know[s] the tune" to sing to Old Man Willow—a tune that can, if necessary, "sing his roots off," or "sing a wind up and blow leaf and branch away."[11] Tom responds to evil not with fear but with the unwavering resolve of one who sees himself as a ruler of the forest, responsible for all the life it contains. His home also serves as a refuge—a place of resilience, community, and love—amid darkness. Tom shows us what it means to "subdue" and to create in a broken world: how to love, steward, and tend without ruthlessness.

We are unlikely to meet and do battle with sinister willows. But we will meet pernicious forces in our world. We may also live in environments that, like Tom's, seem dark and depressing, beyond hope. In the face of these challenges, we can embrace the rhythms of *colere*, its patterns of constancy, love, and fidelity.

We can ask that God would "tune our hearts" aright, and that He would give us words and ways that replenish the world He has made. We can build homes that serve as puddles of heaven in a broken world. To "subdue" becomes an opportunity to mirror God's work in fostering life-giving, relational systems of flourishing. The Creation Mandate's vision of *colere* could apply to the way we design cities, run hospitals, plant and tend our gardens, cook, clean, or parent our children.

In all such instances, the call to cultivate demands the tender care demonstrated in the life of Christ: ministering to tangible, embodied needs in and throughout creation, supporting the proliferation and flourishing of God's webwork of life. In supporting that web, we realize that the voices of nature, as St. Augustine suggests in *Confessions*, are constantly testifying to God's preeminence:

> But what is my God? I put my question to the earth. It answered, "I am not God," and all the things on earth declared the same. I asked the sea and the chasms of the deep and the living things that creep in them, but they answered, "We are not your God. Seek what is above us." I spoke to the winds that blow, and the whole air and all that lives in it replied, "Anaximenes is wrong. I am not God." I asked the sky, the sun, the moon, and the stars, but they told me, "Neither are we the God whom you seek." I spoke to all the things that are about me, all that can be admitted by the door of the senses, and I said, "Since you

are not my God, tell me about Him. Tell me something of my God." Clear and loud they answered, "God is he who made us."[12]

All God's creation, the psalmist reminds us, "declare[s] the glory of God."[13] George MacDonald elucidates this similarly in one of his sermons, in which he writes,

All nature, from the mountains to the sea to the fog that hangs so low on the hills, the heather in August, the hot, the cold, the rain—everything speaks, like the flower, messages from God, the Father of the universe.[14]

The work of cultivation is thus part and parcel of our calling to glorify God and to enjoy Him forever. When we embrace the Creation/Culture Mandate, the lives we cultivate join in a universal chorus. We are no longer out of tune, sleepwalking, unaware of the glory all about us, but listening to and joining in these voices. We participate in a universal song of praise, and take our place in the magnificent dance of the cosmos.

Therefore, friends, let us follow Markel's advice and "go straight into the garden, walk and play there, love, appreciate, and kiss each other, and glorify life."[15]

The Art of Naming

MARILYN MCENTYRE

Like Adam—called by God to name the animals—we have power to meet God in His creative work by naming things. With that power comes responsibility, says writer and teacher Marilyn McEntyre. How should we use it? How might we revitalize the created order, restore what has been eroded, and shape culture toward truth, beauty, and goodness?

My daughters remember a moment when we paused on a walk by a particularly beautiful, deep-purple stand of lobelia. "That's so pretty!" one of them said. "What's it called?" For some reason, at that moment, I couldn't recall its name. "I'm not sure," I replied, a bit abashed. "I'll look it up." But her sister leapt into the breach: "I think I'll call it Ralph," she announced. Her decisiveness and clarity about the matter made us laugh then and still does when we happen to see a bit of lobelia. In our family, I'm afraid, it's still Ralph.

Naming things is a particular pleasure—we begin early with dolls, dogs, now and again a caterpillar or a stray cat (which, once it's been named, becomes a candidate for adoption). Even the smallest children know that bestowing a name establishes a relationship, and that being called by name, and by sundry nicknames and endearments, is a sign and seal of loving connection. Many of them also know that when their full name is called—first, middle, and last—slowly and emphatically, they may be in trouble.

The namer has power; the giver of the name has a claim on the one named. "I have called you by name and you are mine," the Lord proclaims to His people in Isaiah, and that ringing assurance is followed by a promise that reaches back to the Red Sea and forward to Jesus's farewell to His disciples: "When you pass through the waters I will be with you." To have been called by name is to be known, claimed, loved, and sustained, and also to have been summoned into a relationship with profound obligations and consequences.

WHAT'S IN A NAME?

Naming comes up in the Old Testament almost eight hundred times (in the whole of Scripture, nearly a thousand) leaving little question as to its importance. Given names signify character or commemorate life-changing encounters; they're sometimes assigned by divine mandate ("Your name is Israel." "You shall call

his name Ishmael" "…John" "…Jesus") and sometimes changed
as a sign of conversion—Simon to Peter, Saul to Paul. The earliest
instance of God's consigning to humans the pleasure and power
of naming comes in the second chapter of Genesis: "And whatever the man called every living creature, that was its name."

The consequences of the gift of the power to name, for good
and ill, continue to unfold. What we call things changes them.
When we name something, we frame it: we assign it a place
in the Linnaean system of classification or in a family lineage
or in a social hierarchy. We assign people titles and forms of
address that come with access to property or privilege—literal
"entitlement." And we give stories titles that entice or suggest or
foreshadow what will come to matter to us as we step through
the looking glass or wardrobe and suspend disbelief. To read
them is to give hours or days of our time to the ancient quest to
discover what's in a name.

Juliet's famous question, "What's in a name?" is followed by
the self-serving argument that "that which we call a rose / By any
other name would smell as sweet." But the question, meant to
dismiss the power of names, ironically implies its own answer: a
lot lies in a name. A lot is at stake in her impetuous proposal to
Romeo to "Deny thy father and refuse thy name!" A lot is also at
stake in her alternative option: "Or if thou wilt not, be but sworn
my love, / And I'll no longer be a Capulet." For one of these two
young people to give up the family name for the other would
either end or intensify an ancient feud. In this play, Shakespeare,
who fathomed and celebrated the power of words as richly

as any who have wielded them, lays out the tragic potential
of names when they become signifiers for whole histories of
conflict. We have only to consider what has become of names
like *Jezebel* or *Judas, Benedict Arnold* or *Uncle Tom.*

Shakespeare's comedies, on the other hand, turn our attention
to the artful, playful possibilities of naming, usually by way of
re-naming: Rosalind becomes Ganymede and Viola becomes
Cesario, changing not only their names but their gender to teach
their lovers lessons. Playful, though, is not trivial. Here too, a great
deal hangs on the giving and taking of names, and the power
the women claim in *re-naming* themselves for their own purposes
flirts with danger in broaching great cultural taboos. Self-
authorization, especially in women, is at best unsettling to those
deeply anchored in patriarchal traditions, and at worst heretical.

NOT NEUTRAL ENTITIES

We see a variation on this same theme of self-authorization in
The Scarlet Letter when Hester Prynne, finally forgiven by her
harsh judges, refuses to take off the label they sentenced her to
wear, having in effect transformed its meaning with hard-won
irony. She turns her badge of shame into a sign of contradiction,
defying church and state by an act of retranslation.

We see it again in Toni Morrison's unforgettable character
Pilate in *Song of Solomon* who transforms her name—a male
name resonant with betrayal and cowardice—and redeems it,

infusing it with her own meaning on her own terms. Indeed, the title of the novel itself entails a similar ironic reframing of the biblical love poem. Morrison's later novel *Beloved* takes another, perhaps even deeper, look at how naming—or not naming—can change the way we look at both personal and cultural history. Beloved, a child killed by her mother to save her from enslavement, goes to her grave unnamed except for that one descriptor which, some readers have suggested, stands for the many enslaved people whose names have been forgotten, but whose tragic history continues to break, and break open, the hearts of their people.

Among the many literary explorations of the power of naming, Charles Williams's arcane but gripping novel *The Place of the Lion* (1931) occupies a unique, if somewhat marginal, place. A favorite of several of the Oxford Inklings, the novel deals directly and disturbingly with the mysterious power that lies in naming: it is in naming the forces of destruction that Anthony, the protagonist, establishes dominion over them (see Lewis's letter about the book to Arthur Greeves, February 26, 1936).

The story reminds us, lest we moderns have forgotten, that archetypes, angels, Platonic forms, ideas themselves are forces at work in the world and that we negotiate with them at our peril. They are not neutral entities. Nor are words: rather than simple sounds or indicators, words are instruments that control, confine, consign, or perhaps enliven and empower. They kill or heal. When we speak them into the universe, there is an answer.

NAMING AND CLAIMING

These stories (and scores of others) point us toward a question that should, at least from time to time, trouble our sleep: how do we use the power to name? And how might the creative work of re-naming help to bend the arc of history toward justice and the arts of language toward truth? How might any of us use that Adamic authority to revitalize our relationship to the created order? How might re-naming restore what has been eroded or depleted of meaning? And how are we to understand our responsibility for what we have called by name and made our own?

To take the last of those questions first, I would point out that history itself rests on naming and claiming. The way we think and talk about our own countries and societies is based on names that we have inherited, often to the (sometimes violent) exclusion of others. We live in a world after Babel; however we interpret that story, we must conclude that God has allowed our languages to be sundered because of our pride. This was the fall of language, and in this fallen world there is competition between languages—sometimes quite brutal competition. All too often, tyrants exert their power by attempting to rename something and to destroy even the memory of the old names.

As Christians, we have the ability—and the obligation—to look *beyond* the limitations of the naming we see at work in our cultures. We must strive to see what in our culture's naming is true and what is tyrannous. Where is a name an indication of reality, and where is it an attempt to veil reality? Sometimes, of course, a name can be both of these things, and that is where we must use prudence to discern how we use our power of naming to bring justice and true knowledge to our communities.

The opposite of this virtuous naming is when we try to use names—or re-naming—to exert power over reality rather than to discern and reveal a reality that is hidden. For example, throughout history humans have renamed regions as part of conquest; sometimes the re-naming takes place by the stroke of a pen, sometimes by planting a flag, but always with solemn words that assign a new name, one that is often explicitly proprietary: British East Africa; French West Africa; Belgian Congo; Spanish Guinea; German East Africa.

This practice of coercive name-changing makes it easier for invading governments to impose unjust political and social poli-cies. Explorers' and colonizers' assignment of names overlooked or ignored not only the claims but the names given to places indigenous peoples inhabited, including sacred lands. In the case of the examples above, part of the process of establishing national independence and addressing deep-seated injustice has been restoring old names: Kenya, Senegal, Niger, Democratic Republic of the Congo, Rwanda, Mozambique, to mention just a few.

Closer to home, America is still wrestling with the lingering scars of the slave trade, which used un-naming to dehumanize its victims. Slave traders imported ships full of newly nameless people whose identities had been stripped away; to this day, many of their descendants still carry the names of white "owners" or ancestors, a daily reminder of a cruel practice that sought to subjugate and dehumanize an entire group of people.

Addressing these past injustices will require us to face this history of unjust naming. Right now in America there are some efforts to do this; we are seeing waves of re-Africanized names, anonymized last names like Malcolm X, and restoration of indigenous tribal names for land.

NAMING NONHUMAN CREATION

There is a similar movement in science. Right now, there are intriguing, exhilarating, controversial, and consequential efforts taking place among scientists, nature lovers, conservationists, preservationists, and poets to rethink the words we English speakers have used for nonhuman beings. One of the more eloquent apologists for rethinking the way language links us to other creatures is Robin Wall Kimmerer's *Braiding Sweetgrass*. Both a professor of botany and a member of the Potowatomi tribe, Kimmerer organizes her elegant reflections around the central question of how to integrate the insights of empirical science, along with European systems of classification and naming with the insights of tribal peoples who have lived close to their lands for centuries, have known them intimately, and have woven that knowledge into highly poetic, sometimes elliptical, myths and teachings.

How, for instance, might the rich creation story of Sky Woman, who "created a garden for the well-being of all," be reconciled either with the Eden story or with the Enlightenment-influenced, strictly impersonal, descriptive nomenclature of Darwin, von Humboldt, and Mendel? Kimmerer notes that most of her graduate students, invested as they are in learning, have lost a connection she longs to restore: "when they put more energy into memorizing Latin names," she observes, "they spend less time looking at the beings themselves."

Kimmerer's book is more invitational than critical; indeed she expresses great respect for what she has learned in the lab from highly skilled plant scientists. But she also invites readers to a kind of humility that reaches to the root of that word—*humus,* which becomes a word for soil. Humility calls us to return to our own sensate, elemental relationship with soil, strawberries, and squash not primarily as products to be purchased but as gifts given to be enjoyed in a context of gratitude and reciprocity. She uses words like "community" and "relatives" to describe the plant lives with which humans interact, and brings what one science writer called "the tenderness of the scientific gaze" to bear on those beings' habits and needs and strategies of survival.

"In some Native languages," Kimmerer points out, by way of example, "the term for plants translates to 'those who take care of us.'" Imagine what might shift if we were simply to shift the pronoun we use to describe a tree from "what" to "who" or spoke of "cows" rather than "livestock."

The culture of commodification seeks to drive a wedge between our relationship with things as creatures and our experience of those things as goods. It does this by introducing

separate terms: one set that identifies living beings as creatures—participants in creation—and a whole separate set that
identifies them as marketable products. Jesus's parable of the
shepherd who leaves the ninety-nine sheep to find and rescue
the hundredth suggests a kind of caring that remains relational,
even though lambs were sold, slaughtered, and eaten. The use of
the names "sheep" and "lamb" remind us that we have a relationship—and responsibilities—to these animals, even though we
may end up eating them.

MAPPING THE WORLD

Non-human beings have their own ways of being—even their
ways of knowing. They have, as botanist Peter Wohlleben put it,
a "hidden life." Knowing their secrets takes time and patience,
and some relinquishment of anthropocentric assumptions. And
this knowing requires new words, foreign or poetic or sometimes
fanciful, to get at how other creatures, our leafy protectors and
those Thoreau called our "brute neighbors," live and move and
have their being.

Tolkien provided some of that in his sweeping story of
a time when Middle Earth included many orders of living
beings—dwarves and hobbits and elves and Ents as well as
humans—whose coexistence was a working relationship rooted
in an understanding of complementarity. Each kind of being in
Middle Earth has a distinctive language, its sounds and rhythm

and range of reference suited to their character and work. Elvin
speech is marked by fluid loveliness. Words and names like
Ainulindale, Anarya, Dunedain, Galadriel, Lothlorien, Namarie,
and Tauriel are as close as language comes to music. Dwarves,
on the other hand, have consonant-rich, hard-edged words like
zirakzigil, gabilgathol, narag, and baruk.

   This is no accident. As both a philologist and a man of deep
faith, Tolkien brought a sensibility to his work that drew upon
the ancient Hebrew understanding of naming as something I
would call, in Christian terms, sacramental. He also understood
and conveyed how words distinguish the way groups of people
see the world and what they care for. Common words, as well
as names, map our relationship with the world. We live inside
grammatical structures that organize and give meaning to what
is given. Tolkien's fiction and his more scholarly philological
studies all point to a fact that should continue to inform our
curricula: linguistic diversity, like biodiversity, is a prerequisite for
a healthy planet. Our complementarity and the patient, nuanced
work of translation keep us in a field of creative tension as we
work out our means of production and our hopes for peace.

KNOWN ONLY BY GOD

Clearly—as Tolkien knew, and as Kimmerer reminds us—we
share this lovely, fragile earth, "our island home," with creatures
who know things we don't. In one of his unusually lighthearted

poems, T. S. Eliot offers a reminder not to assume that the names
we impose on those creatures are in any way a final measure of
who's there.

The opening lines of "The Naming of Cats" introduces the
problem: "The naming of cats is a difficult matter, / It isn't just
one of your holiday games ..." The speaker goes on to explain
with comic earnestness that a cat must have (as he emphasized
in all caps) THREE DIFFERENT NAMES. In addition to the
"sensible, everyday names" a cat keeper (I hesitate to say owner)
might give, and a name that's "peculiar and more dignified," there
is "that name that no human research can discover— / but THE
CAT HIMSELF KNOWS and will never confess."

I quote here the last lines of the poem with some reluctance,
since to do so offers a kind of spoiler when I'd rather you hasten
to your bookshelf or, if you must, the internet and spend a few
delightful minutes with the entire poem:

> When you notice a cat in profound meditation,
>   The reason, I tell you, is always the same:
> His mind is engaged in a rapt contemplation
>   Of the thought, of the thought, of the thought of his
> name:
>   His ineffable effable
>   Effanineffable
> Deep and inscrutable singular name.[1]

The poem still makes me smile after many readings at the
way it takes delight in lists of improbable names and invention

of "effanineffable." It also, perhaps more importantly, makes me remember, when I see the neighborhood stray cat touring our garden, that there is a "who" there, known only to God. And it shores up my conviction that the same is true for us: the one who calls us by name knows that name, even though we ourselves do not.

ECHOES OF THE WORD

Paying attention to words and their effects upon the material and spiritual orders we inhabit is surely part of our calling as people of faith. More particularly, it is a vocation for those among us who, following a desire of the heart given at some early point in our journeys, spend many of our waking hours with words. When we sit at our desks moving words around, it is good to remember that we do this work for the glory of God and the fullness of creation; in every community, there must be some who "wrestle with words and meanings." There must be some who excavate etymologies as there must be archaeologists who dig through layers of ancient soil to help link us to the cultures that have shaped us.

There must be some who ponder the shades of meaning between near-synonyms—the difference between *perplexity* and *confusion*, for instance, or between *settlement* and *occupation*. There must be some—many—who look upon brand names and ad copy with a jaundiced eye and an informed understanding of how "influencers" turn *meaning* into *manipulation*. And there must be many who cherish the words we inscribe in life-giving liturgy and poetry and prayer.

Cherishing does not prevent us from retranslating from time to time; instead, it calls us to hold on to what is good, to pay our tithe of due attention to sacred texts as they summon us to "lift up our hearts," and to join in the joyful noise of a thousand tongues that daily pray their versions of "hallowed be thy name"—a line that begins in Aramaic with a summoning to "Hear the one sound that created all others."[2]

The reality of words is that they are always mere echoes of the great Word. Because of this, speaking true words begins and ends with listening.

The Art of Subcreation

MATTHEW CLARK

God's eternal Great Story is unfolding in time, and singer-songwriter Matthew Clark reminds us that we each are part of its telling. In fact, we are invited to collaborate in the storytelling in what Tolkien called subcreation, improvising with elements of Creation as collaborators in a grand drama.

Like many folks, I started and stopped Tolkien's *The Silmarillion* many times before I finally read through the whole thing. I felt a little ashamed; I had been a fan of *The Lord of the Rings* since childhood. But my experience is not uncommon. It's been suggested that *Rings* is easier than *Silmarillion* because the former was written in the community of the Inklings.[1] Thus, *Rings*'s prose is somewhat softened, whereas the *Silmarillion* is full-on Tolkienic diction in all of its glorious (and at times intimidating) density. Sometimes I jokingly think of *The Lord of the Rings* as the easier-to-read "New Testament," and *The Silmarillion* as the challenging "Old Testament"—the backstory we'd rather skim than labor to understand.

However, to extend my joke a little, it is not possible to fully comprehend the "New Testaments" without spending time in the "Old Testaments," in all their thorny glory. At this point I've read through *The Silmarillion* several times. In many ways, reading Tolkien's subcreated creation myth limbered up my imagination to re-encounter the primary "Creation Myth" given to us in Genesis. Tolkien, among others, awakened a taste for something I thought too delicious, too rich to be real—but, miraculously, is free for the taking.

The book you have in your hands, dear reader, aims to recover some of that forgotten richness of the Christian faith. There are many reasons any one of us may have put aside Christianity, like I did *The Silmarillion* for so long, and lost our place in God's Great Story. Perhaps it was the mere strangeness of the literature, the endless hard-to-pronounce names; maybe we were told that stories like this weren't for grown-ups; maybe the beauty was too heartbreaking; or maybe someone used the story to hurt us and we couldn't tell the difference between our trespassers and the God they misrepresented. (If this sounds like you, I want to say that I'm sorry. I'm sorry that this great joy was taken from you. And I want you to know that your place in the most beautiful of tales—the tale we most long to find is true[2]—awaits you still.)

But the Story is true—this world is going somewhere. Through our lives and actions, the Story is this moment continuing to unfold; each of us is enfolded into the telling. Tolkien's term for this is subcreation; by God's design, we are to be real collaborators with and under our Creator. There's something incredible going on here—a *telos* beyond imagining, and God is calling upon your imagination and mine to play a real part in its development. For "whether we speak of poems or places, all art acknowledges an absence and dreams of something other, something more. Art is the material form of hope."[3]

Tolkien understood this in a deep way. And through his understanding he has accompanied me, like Virgil accompanied Dante, through the hell of having lost any sense of who God is and what He's really up to (and what we have been gloriously invited to be up to *with* Him).

THE MAKER OF EARTH *AND* HEAVEN

There I was, in an old 1970s fellowship hall, sitting in a gray metal folding chair in a horseshoe of fake-wood tables. My buddy Oliver was teaching an adult Bible study; I was in town visiting. He was squeaking out teaching points onto a dry-erase board for a handful of parishioners (plus one traveling singer/ songwriter). Then he said something that just about made me spew my watery Folgers onto my neighboring octogenarian. He said, "God created the earth *and* the heavens. This created cosmos contains them *both*."

Heaven is just as much a part of the Creation as earth? How had I missed this fantastical detail? The visible and the invisible were created together, for each other. Even now, they dance in and

out of one another, destined to be wedded in the fullness of time.[4]
When we consider the heavens and all that God has made, we say,
"Lord, what is mankind that You would pay us any attention?"[5]

Before that question leaves our lips, the answer is already
welling up from unseen depths that call out to our depths, where
eternity has been set in our hearts: what we *are* is something
from beyond the material making its appearance in materiality.[6]
Home is the heart of God, said George MacDonald, and though
we find ourselves situated in the material world, we sense rightly
that we originate from beyond mere materiality. Man's true
nature is supernatural.[7]

If you want evidence that the spiritual affects the physical
and vice versa, you carry the proof with you under your hat. I can
read the state of your spirit in the expression of your face, the
sound of your laughter, or the presence of tears on your cheeks.
And it works in the other direction too. I can feel the kindness
on your face make its way to mine where a smile forms—a smile
that soaks down past flesh and bone and brightens my very
spirit. Here, the micro clues us into the macro; the whole cosmos
plays along this same pattern, allowing us to read into the material and discover in it something of what lies beyond it.

INTELLIGENCE AS A PRACTICE

Widespread literacy is a relatively recent thing. To most people
for most of time, the writing on a scroll or the pages of a book

was not legible. Squiggles, scratches, loops and lashes did not cohere to reveal any meaning at all. Thus, as Jim Henson put it, "When people told themselves their past with stories, explained their present with stories, foretold the future with stories, the best place by the fire was kept for the storyteller."[8]

In those days, however, another "book" lay open to them: the world itself. Upon its living pages, people could read much about the nature and dreams of the world's Author. In his epistle to the Romans, St. Paul warns those who disregard what's written in creation, saying that because of what *is* legible there, we cannot pretend that we didn't know.

Against this background, our calling as subcreators goes against society's view of creativity. If you're like me, the word "originality" piles on pressure. I tend to think of *myself* as the origin of originality: *I've got to come up with something no one has ever thought of before!* But as subcreators, we don't need to carry that burden; originality does not mean creating our own meaning but rather returning to our Origin: God.

The Romantic movement tried to respond to the removal of God (and transcendence in general) from the world after the Enlightenment and in the midst of the Industrial Revolution. Naturalism became the new religion, and it reduced the world to mere material. The Romantics took it upon themselves to assign meaning and purpose, through their art, to a world daily becoming more estranged from its Origin—an estrangement that trickled down through modernism, postmodernism, and continues today.[9]

For us, subcreative "originality" works very differently, as we practice training our senses, imaginations, and minds upon the legibility of the world. This practice might be called intelligence or "reading-into" as I described in a previously published work and quote here:

> A right understanding of the word *intelligence* is relevant here. The word breaks down like this: *intus* (into) + *legere* (to read), "which means to read or understand into a thing, *to penetrate the interior quality of a thing with one's mind*." For me it is encouraging to learn that intelligence is not a passive trait one has or doesn't have; it is rather an active discipline one practices, a discipline of looking closely, listening and attending with care, and learning to read and receive the truth of a thing's being or essence as it has been invested there by God. Tolkien was not automatically intelligent and therefore able to "break the veil"; he was deeply invested in the long work of "reading into the reality of things" primarily, in his case, by attending to words. I can't help but think of Jesus as *The Word* through whom all things were made …[10]

Recovering intellect as a practice may offer a road to recovering a way of seeing ourselves and this world not as a mass of material but as continually unfolded from the heart of the Trinity. Though loving God with all our mind is involved, intelligence is not primarily about being smart; it's about becoming wise to Reality through a prayerful posture of attentiveness. It's far more about receptivity than anything like achievement, and therefore is not exclusive to brainy types. Before we begin any work of subcreation, we must practice this kind of intelligence, this "*reading-into*" the world God has made, discovering its Logos there: Jesus. Jesus is the meaning of the cosmos. He is its rationale, its origin, and its destiny.

MAKING TO SEE

We've identified the problem of failing to *read-into* Reality. But what now? Josef Pieper says we must learn to see again. To do this, first we need to abstain from mere noise: the cacophony that distracts us from distraction by more distraction, as T. S. Eliot says. However, abstaining leaves a house swept clean, but empty. It's a start, but we can't stop there. Pieper goes on:

> A better and more immediately effective remedy is this:
> to be active oneself in artistic creation, producing shapes
> and forms for the eye to see.
>
> Nobody has to observe and study the visible
> mystery of the human face more than the one who sets
> out to sculpt it in a tangible medium. . . . Before you can
> express anything in tangible form, you first need eyes to
> see. The mere attempt, therefore, to create an artistic form
> compels the artist to take a fresh look at the visible reality;
> it requires authentic and personal observation.[11]

Making art is a way to carry on the practice of intelligence we've been talking about. The result is that the house, swept clean and emptied of all that diabolic chaos, is "re-cosmos-ed" and filled with Logos as we work at our craft. Jacques Maritain can thus describe art as a virtue of the *practical intellect*[12] that transforms artists as they work at their craft: a virtuous cycle is maintained as "they are, in a way, their work before they create it: to be able to form it, they have conformed to it."[13]

All of that reorients us to creativity not as something we command but as something we conform to, something that transforms and even sanctifies us as we practice it. The making makes us, as we meet with our Maker in the making.

Along these same lines, Andy Crouch has pointed out that culture is not an abstract thing; rather, it is made out of things.[14] If you want to affect culture, for instance, you need to make stuff. So think about how God does things: He's made a world of things, which stand as an invitation to *read-into* (intelligence) the world's given meaning, inviting us into a real participation in the Life of the Trinity. God has not primarily approached us through abstract arguments, has He? Even the portions of Scripture that may get labeled abstract arguments—Romans and Hebrews, for example— are rich narrative recollections meant to further open the mysteries[15] being made available through a culture of preserved story.

Roger Lundin says ours is a narrative God, known through the things He's made and the things He does.[16] Of course philo- sophical exploration and long mental meanderings are invited to the party, but we're not, in the end, trying to capture an idea. We are looking to touch a Face. As subcreators, we are ever searching for "the light of the knowledge of the glory of God in the *face* of Christ." Next, we partner with God as we work, within the givenness of things, to re-wed what has been put asunder. But we don't just restore things to some prior, static state. God has initiated something dynamic. We also work to fulfill latent possibilities, developing surprising realities that, though new, inhere with the original intent of the Logos. This is subcreation.

NAMING: LOVING IN ORDER TO KNOW

Right naming knits true correspondences together. Misnomers put reality out of reach, and the consequences can be deadly. We see it all through the Gospels as Jesus's detractors fail to discern His true name. They refuse to see Him truly. Likewise, name-calling (whether it's against ourselves or others) can be devastating; we long to hear our Lord gracefully, mercifully name us His Beloved. Naming locates us in a relationship out of which a storyline can unfold, and every story attempts to name us.

We must become aware of those stories and be deliberate about which ones we practice. We're constantly being offered false names that pull us off into other storylines, and those storylines include practices (liturgies) that shape our desires, our sense of what is possible, even the terms or names by which we understand ourselves in relation to everything and everyone. As subcreators, we are involved in naming. One of the earliest invitations from God to get us involved in His work had to do with naming the animals. This was not an invitation to assign arbitrary linguistic signifiers as we saw fit[17]; it was a sacred invitation to read-into the essence of each creature, to discover there its given being. To love it well in order to know it truly.[18] Having rightly discerned what that thing actually *was*, we were to craft a linguistic point of contact with the truth of the thing, a Name.

I can't remember who said that the hardest thing to do is say what you mean. Naming is like that. Subcreation is like that. We need the Holy Spirit's help to lead us into all truth, if we're to name faithfully. The work of reading-into the reality of things and then articulating that through some medium (words, clay, imagery, etc.) is hard, worthy work. Look around you and you'll see many wonderful results of humanity's response to the call. Someone lovingly looked into grapes and by rightly discerning their essence, added to their name, wine. Someone held wheat dear enough to attend to its God-embedded reality, and added to its name, bread.

What happens when the Creator draws our subcreative namings up into His creative name-giving potency? The One who, in saying names, realizes them by His power? ("Let there be light!") Well, things like the Eucharist happen: the given things (wheat and grapes) become a human-crafted "name" (bread and wine), and are given back to God, who extends their names, realizing them as a means of contact and union with Himself.

Likewise, through the gift of Jesus's incarnation, death, and resurrection, the true name of humanity is further developed. By becoming one of us, Jesus has applied His craft to the human raw materials He created in the first place, further unfolding humanity's given potency. He makes of us a Beloved Bride (a name we've hardly begun to understand), temples of the Holy Spirit, even a City (suggestive of the heights of human subcreativity).

SUBCREATION AS REUNITING REALITY

A couple of years ago, I heard Ken Myers, founder and host of the *Mars Hill Audio Journal* make an astonishing word connection. In the following quote, Myers is playing with the word "diabolical," and he begins with diabolical's surprising opposite: symbolical.

> [Diabolical and symbolical] both come from the Greek verb "ballein," "to throw." We get our word ball from the same word. The preposition "syn" or "sym" means "together with." The Greek verb symbolo literally means "to throw together, to collect, to join or unite, or to come together." The Christian Creeds were known as the symbols of faith, not merely in the sense that they represented the faith, but that they were a means by which Christians were united.
>
> The verb "diabolo" by contrast means literally "to throw apart, to set at variance, to separate."[19]

Myers points out that the sentences "the creeds *unite* Christians" and "the creeds *symbolize* Christians" are saying the same thing; the verbs *unite* and *symbolize* have the same meaning here.

Alexander Schmemann puts it this way,

> The primary meaning of "symbol" is in no way equivalent
> to "illustration" ... today we understand the symbol as the
> representation or sign of an absent reality (just as there
> is no real, actual water in the chemical symbol H2O),
> in the original understanding it is the manifestation
> and presence of the other reality—which, under given
> circumstances, cannot be manifested and made present
> in any other way than as a symbol.[20]

Interesting, right? Symbolical means to unite; diabolical means to divide. Can you hear it in El Diablo? Even *devil* and *Satan* share the same root word. So let's play with these two words for a few minutes to see how they might outline the work God is calling us to.

We begin with the interlaced life of a Three-Personed God; we find an uncreated symbol at the very beginning: The Trinity. This God creates an angelic host including Lucifer, the "Angel of Light," who for a time enjoys some kind of participation in the Life of the Trinity, until he attempts to name himself God and is cast out of heaven. He is rightly renamed: El Diablo, the Devil.

WEAVING A BETTER TALE

God creates the Cosmos we know and live in. The modern term
"cosmetics" is related to the word *cosmos*. Using cosmetics, a
woman may "order her appearance," and when God *cosmoses*,
He is ordering His creation into a meaningful, integrated wholeness. Though marred by insubordination, creation remains a vast
symbolic manifestation of God's "invisible qualities"[21] and bears
yet His embedded intention. Though we've lost a lot of our skill at
detecting it, its *givenness* is kept intact in Christ.

Enter El Diablo, the Destroyer. From the moment the Lord
said, "Let there be light," the devil's dark way has ever been to
contra-dict what God has dictated. Chaos is anti-cosmos and
anti-symbolic. The Lord sends His creative word out, and El
Diablo works to deconstruct whatever structure the Lord builds,
to destabilize whatever God establishes.

At Sinai, God unites (or symbolizes) a rescued rabble of slave
tribes into a nation-family. Yahweh sews them into the familial
fabric, while the devil pulls at the threads. Eventually, out of
Israel comes a messiah, Jesus. Our Lord has permanently joined
Himself to us in the symbolical act of Incarnation to *re*-member
(as opposed to *dis*-member) humanity and all creation to the
Life of the Trinity. In Christ, the diabolical dividing wall of
hostility between Jew, Gentile, slave and free, man and woman is
abolished.

The devil continually works to shred the storybook and obscure its happy ending, but Jesus is weaving a better tale around us. It's a story that offers a *symbolic* reality; for people in the terrifying free-fall of storylessness, Jesus (along with His fisherman buddies!) has mended a net to catch us and set us down on solid ground. The torn and scattered pages are being carefully gathered and rebound by the Author Himself, becoming a Book of Life. A Book whose most beautiful endless-ending is written in the ink-blood of the Lamb who was slain.

The story Jesus is writing is *symbolic*, which by now you realize doesn't mean less-than-real, but rather that this story reunites us with Reality, making wholeness available. Sure, El Diablo may be trying to unravel the fabric, always and ever "putting asunder what God has joined together." But, rest assured that in the end, humanity will be symbolized to God. Which is the same as saying, Jesus shall be wedded to His dearly bought Bride.

You see, then, my fellow subcreators, we have good reason to be courageous in our calling! A chosen Cornerstone has been laid, and upon it a new symbol is taking shape—an Everlasting Family. God's judgment will mend all things, stitching the stranded threads again into a seamless fabric. We're already picking up on the patterns and getting involved. But it's not easy; you don't need me to tell you how frustrating the (sub)creative process can be! We look into a clouded mirror. For now, we live in the diabolical separation between God's promised reality and our experience of brokenness. The betrothal period is no fun, but heaven and earth will be married one day. The gap between how things are and how they should be shall close, and we shall see Him face to Face.

That's our situation, broadly speaking. You see, then, our opportunity? God is calling us to join Him in this symbolizing work whereby the sundered creation is rejoined to its Creator. Heaven and Earth, God and Mankind, visible and invisible, immanent and transcendent, thing and name: *wedded.* Amazingly, it is through us that He means to accomplish this.

Shall we extend our little etymological adventure? Want to guess another word built with some of the same bits as symbolic and diabolic? Remember: *sym*-ballein (to throw together) and *dia*-ballein (to throw apart)? Think of what parable and *para*bolic mean, and *para*-ballein (to throw alongside). Jesus uses parables and the art of storytelling to take sundered meanings and toss them alongside one another. For those willing to read-into His narrative creations, the undoing of the diabolic becomes available: the amnesiac bride is remembered with her true name.[22]

As subcreators we search out the patterns embedded in the givenness of Creation, learn those stories, and like Tolkien's Niggle, paint our little "leaves"—whether they be a song, a poem, a play, a meal, a family, a conversation, a book. Thus is the hard ground of disenchantment softened and nourished by a thousand parables, the air filled by the dance of a thousand symbols each holding in themselves a light from beyond the walls of the world. This is a Story older than the world, yet new in each telling.[23]

ICONS VS. IDOLS

Every "telling" we put forth in a subcreated artifact works like
an icon. Icons subvert idolatry, because their work is to invite all
who meet them to set their hearts on pilgrimage (see Psalm 84:5).
Icons draw us into and through themselves toward the One to
whom they bear witness. Every beautiful thing humbly confesses,
"No, not me," calling us to follow its beauty further, saying,
"He fathers-forth whose beauty is past change: Praise Him."[24]

Idols, in contrast, demand that we cease our pilgrimage of
beholding[25] that moves us ever onward to the Beatific Vision, that
Joy set before us: the face-to-Face meeting with Jesus that is the
destiny which through us the cosmos shares in. Idols say, "Stop
here, I'll be your god."

As subcreators, we set our hearts on pilgrimage, rejecting
idols, crafting icons that draw us and others back into the story
God is telling.

OF AULE AND THE
MAKING OF DWARVES

Remember our mention of *The Silmarillion*? Now's as good a time
as any to tell you a favorite story from that tome. I think you'll see
how it relates to what we've been talking about.

Once upon a time, Eru Ilúvatar created Middle Earth. He had
first revealed it in a Great Music to his servants the Valar, whose

voices, at Eru's invitation, were joined to his, to labor alongside him within his own themes. One Valar, in his pride, sought to sow discord; but, Eru, all-wise, ever incorporated the discordancy into new and surprising music of even greater depth and beauty. At length, all of the Valar were given a Vision of Eru's song, realized before them in the void, and Eru told them that whomever would, could go down into the creation and abide there to nurture it. Some of the Valar did. But when they reached Middle Earth, they were surprised to find it undeveloped.

The Vision they'd seen was of the world's potential not yet achieved. There the world lay unpeopled, though Ilúvatar had promised the eventual arrival of the Children his mind alone had conceived. Ever attuned to the music of Eru, the Valar delighted in their work; all their powers were called upon to wake and shape the rudiment world before them until the Song would be well-wrought, whether in wood, stone, or water.

But Aulë grew impatient for the arrival of the Children of Ilúvatar, and in secret places shaped the dwarves. For he wished that there might be ones other than himself to whom to teach his craft, lore, and to love. Ilúvatar knew what was done, and that hour spoke to Aulë, saying, "Why have you done what is beyond your power and authority?" Aulë, being only a subcreator, had not the power to bestow true being upon his dwarves, and so they would only ever exist as puppets.

In humility, Aulë repented, confessing his haste and folly. Yet his intentions were true-hearted, for he said to Ilúvatar, "the making of things is in my heart from my own making by thee, and the child of little understanding that makes a play of the deeds of his father may do so without thought of mockery."

He went on, "As a child to his father, I offer you these things, the work of the hands which thou hast made." Then, hating his own presumption, Aulë lifted up his hammer to destroy them. But the Creator had compassion on him and his desire. Ilúvatar stopped Aulë and, further, granted true being and personhood to the dwarves. When Aulë saw this, he threw down his hammer and was glad; he said, "May Eru bless my work and amend it!" Thus was the desire and handiwork of humble Aulë (whose name means "maker") taken up by the Creator and given life and place in the World.[26]

I love that little scene. The whole structure of Tolkien's mythic Secondary World is shaped by his understanding of subcreation in our Primary World, and the Aulë account warns us against inordinate making[27] while also expanding our wildest hopes about how our sub(missive) creating might be drawn up into the Life of the Trinity. Idols may be transformed into icons. Who knows how the True God might take up, bless, and amend the few warbling notes we add to the Song, the few measly sentences we offer to the Great Storybook, the one little leaf we paint of the Tree, giving to them a life beyond our power to realize a Story only His mind has conceived?

WISE IN THE SPIRIT:
JAZZ AND DRAMA

For we are people of *that* Story, living in a world that has lost
its story. We began this chapter noting how we've been trained
since the eighteenth-century Enlightenment to see the world as
merely material without any real participation in a transcendent
reality. This idea is a very recent historical phenomenon. The vast
majority of humans up until just a few hundred years ago auto-
matically thought of themselves as being a part of a meaningful
cosmic storyline. But guess what? There's an anti-story story.
There is a story that says there is no story. That's the story our world
believes today. This is worth grasping: *Unbelief is itself a belief in
a particular story that says there is no story.*[28]

In general, this anti-story story has enslaved our culture's
imagination, draining the world of its God-given significance.
Significance has to do with signs (*semeia*[29]) that signal a
Signature, and a signature is the personal handwriting of a
Living Person with a Name. That Signature has effectively been
erased for most folks, and so the world has no storyline—no
creator from whom it came, no redeemer to whom it is moving in
hope and promise. This dramatic decontextualization of human
characters is what creates the terrifying free-fall of storylessness
I mentioned earlier.

But Christianity has always taught that Jesus Himself is the
One through and for whom the Cosmos was created. He is the
Word, the Logos, the basis of its reality; again, the meaning of

the world *is* Jesus. And the ongoing dramatic unfolding of the world's story is the work of the Father, Son, and Holy Spirit in its Creation, Redemption, and re-making.

We have a place in that Great Story. We came from, and are going to, somewhere good; we are swathed in meaning-rich context. In this "middle act," we are invited to be God's collaborators. How do we find our place in this Story as subcreators? If the Lamb's Book of Life is not a ledger sheet but a Grand Storybook endlessly unfolding, "in which every chapter is better than the one before,"[30] how do we join in its telling with our very lives? I'd like to look at two intertwining analogies: drama and jazz.

Let's start with Hans Urs von Balthasar's play analogy. Balthasar says the Father has laid out a script (which is His Will), sent the Principal Actor onto the stage (Jesus), and presently the Holy Spirit is acting as the play's director, overseeing the action, even inviting the audience up onto the stage to participate in the enactment of the drama. So again, the Father is the Playwright, the Son is the Principal Actor, and the Holy Spirit is the Director.

What's the first thing an actor has to do if she's going to be in a play? She had better put in the time to memorize the script. The Script is God's will—the Script is the *Script*ures. There's no clever gimmick here; if you want to get the story of God's will into your bones, read the Bible every day, pray, and bodily rehearse with other believers in worship.

Because the Story that God is telling *has* been made available, we can avail ourselves of this resource. God's will is not a certain rock in a certain field in a certain town where you must stand on one foot. Rather, it is a vast realm of righteousness where God is working out a particular drama in His Cosmos through the One in whom the Cosmos subsists, Jesus.

What is the story that God is telling? We've already spent time outlining it above in terms of symbolic and diabolic. If you can get that story down, you'll see where the world came from and where it's all going, and this whole world (and you) will be situated in a context that will allow you to understand its meaning so that you can live creatively attuned to God's intentions for it. The fact is, you are being invited out of the audience and onto the stage to enact the Father's Script, getting your cues from the Principal Actor, Jesus, while following the directions of the Holy Spirit.

Now here's something I think is fascinating and wonderful. The more and more deeply familiar you become with the Script of the play (Bible reading, worship), the stronger your rapport with the Principal Actor becomes (prayer, obedience), and the more attentive you become to the Director's instructions (prayer, fellowship in the Body of Christ), the freer you become to *play* within the play—in other words, to improvise.

David Ford says that "our knowledge of a culture is revealed by what to do or say next. In the drama of living, the deepest understanding is shown in the wisest improvisation."[31] Improvisation is a species of wisdom that enables an actor to respond to all kinds of circumstances in a way that stays true to the script. It's based on character. Righteousness is God's character (and He never breaks character). As we are conformed to Jesus's likeness, we are dressing up as Christ, we are "putting on" God's storyline, getting into costume, into character.

The irony with this particular play is that when you dress up and make-believe you are likely to feel inauthentic. Why? Because sin has worked an anti-story story into this world and made us all, in traditional Greek dramatic terms, hypocrites: false-faced mask-wearers. However, to follow Jesus is to learn to live truthfully again on the stage of reality: to grow true faces. You're actually becoming more and more true, more real, more yourself.[32] We are being prepared for a meeting with Reality, and, as Lewis says, we can't meet face to Face "till we have faces."[33]

Meanwhile, the joy of improvisation is that the Script takes on a life of its own through each actor's unique gifts and personality. That's why you can see the wonderful vitality, abundance, and variation of faithful Christianity around the world through improvisations on praise music, dance, instrumentation, architecture, food, and dress. You can see endless iterations of Christ's actions across the centuries as faithful followers have lived, served, and died in wildly creative ways.

SING AND STIR THE UNSEEN

St. Augustine said, "Love God and do what you will." In other words, the play is not scripted in a meticulous, deterministic sense. You've got the Script—get it into your bones, keep your eyes on the lead actor, listen for directions, and from there, just riff on the themes, improvise. Have fun.

Which brings me to a final analogy I love as a musician, and that's musical improvisation. It works the same way. Any jazz musician's goal is improvisation, but it takes years of training on scales, absorbing a traditional repertoire of tunes, learning to follow a conductor, and so on. All that work to familiarize yourself with that tradition means that at any moment the band leader might call you up onto the stage to jam and you can respond instantly. Duke Ellington can randomly point to his trumpeter Cootie Williams and say, "Take a solo," and Cootie steps right into the long stream of jazz's storyline and adds to the music. He speaks the language as naturally and freely as the wind blows.

It's like that for us. Maybe we can't relate to the play analogy or imagine ourselves jamming with the jazz band, but surely almost everyone can relate to speaking to someone in a conversation. There was a time when you couldn't talk. You spent years learning the language, picking up phrases, idioms, reading books, practicing within the tradition of your mother tongue, and unless you're literally reading off a page, you are improvising speech almost constantly. The fact that you can have a conversation that is intelligible to another human means that you are improvising in a way that is true to the storyline of that linguistic tradition, which is serving as a kind of script or song within which speakers improvise.

Dear friends, this world is about something. It has a storyline. It has a Storyteller who is calling us up onto the stage to subcreatively contribute to this unfolding drama, to play a trumpet solo on the instrument of our very lives within the song God is singing over us. As Tolkien wrote, "I would that I might with the minstrels sing and stir the unseen with a throbbing string!"[34]

COSMIC YOKEFELLOWS

Tolkien's creation myth in *The Silmarillion* begins with the deity, Eru Ilúvatar, propounding a cosmos (through song no less!) to his created helpers, the Valar; but when they reach the nascent Middle Earth, though all the materials are in place, the vision is unfinished. It is up to them to develop it, through subcreation. As we watch the Valar work amongst themselves under the direction of Eru's Vision, Tolkien's invented tale clues us into our Christian subcreative calling. They must also contend creatively with rebellious subcreators, like Melkor and Sauron, who mar[35] and pervert (there can be no *per*version without a Primary *Version*) by foul craft.

Likewise, the True God of Primary Reality has created this cosmos out of nothing (*ex nihilo*) and deliberately left room for us to join Him in its continual unfolding and development. This Cosmos is the perfect shop class wherein humanity might be apprenticed to the Master Creator, learning the trade of world-building (perhaps even literally[36]). Sadly, humanity only got one or two classes in before we flunked out. Perhaps, when it comes to our capability, limitations have been placed on fallen humanity (what responsible father hands the Corvette keys to the toddler?), yet the invitation remains to "make still by the law in which we're made."[37] As Christians we even "participate in the divine nature"[38] of an everlastingly fecund Trinity.

We are makers and artists, yes. But I particularly appreciate this term "subcreator" that Tolkien has coined for us, because it highlights our incorporation, our felicitous enfolding into the life and work of the Trinity. We work *under*, *with,* and *in* our Creator to realize with Him, through every imaginative endeavor at making, a Vision so vast and glorious that "no eye has seen, no ear has heard, and no human mind has conceived"[39] its end. We who have never known a tree gaze dreamily at mustard seeds.

Be assured: we were made for this: to be *with* and *like* our God. And whatever unimaginably glorious work He is up to, we've been created to labor in its realization with Him—to be yoked together with the Logos Himself, the very Word through whom all worlds were made and in whom worlds yet to be made await.

Why We Create:
The Eucharistic Life

JEROMIE RAND

*There's a reason for the threefold creative
process—in which God creates, we create, and
God meets us in the creation and transforms
it into a means of grace. The reason, says
Father Jeromie Rand, is the linchpin of what
it means to be a creative person—which is
to say, what it means to be human.*

Arapahoe Community College, where I teach, was built during
the Brutalist period of architecture. People who drive by and don't
read the sign out front think it's a prison. I spend most of my
workday in a portion of the building that has no windows, so I
go into this gigantic concrete enclosure and I have no idea what's
happening outside.

This building is proclaiming one of the underlying narratives
of our culture: that beauty is unnecessary, and function is all that
matters. This building proclaims one of the underlying narratives
of our culture. What are its tenets? That truth is relative, and we

cannot know whether something participates in the good, the true, and the beautiful, or whether it is ugly and false. That there is a wall between the sacred and the secular, and no one—religious or secular—should cross that wall.

Oftentimes, our churches reinforce these messages. The sanctuaries are stripped and ugly; only functional things are left; and anything that does not explicitly communicate the gospel has no place in the church.

FIGHTING FALSE NARRATIVES

This is the heresy the Church faces today: the false narrative that there is some kind of dividing wall between heaven and earth, and between our work here on earth and our eternal salvation. This heresy attacks not only our identity as citizens of heaven but also our purpose and joy here on earth.

The truth is that God places us in this world as a gift so that we might learn about Him through it. We are not made for this world, but it is made for us. It exists to reveal God to us.

And there is more. Not only does this world exist for us, but it exists to be shaped by us—and the shapes we make of it, the new things we add to existence, can reveal God to others. This is what Tolkien means when he says that we are "subcreators": That we, by participating in God's image as creators, can actually contribute to the revelation of God's nature.

Now, a little doctrinal clarification here: there are two kinds of revelation, the *special* revelation of God's Word and the *general* revelation of nature. We are *not* contributing to what God has revealed to us through His Word. Between the Scriptures and the Person of Christ (God's literal Word, according to the Gospel of John), God's special revelation is complete. It is the task of the Church to steward that revelation and to discern, through the Holy Spirit, how to apply it to situations as they arise, but not to add to it.

GOD SHOWING HIMSELF

General revelation is a little different. Like its name implies, general revelation is not as specific, and not as theologically helpful, as special revelation. But it is crucial in forming our imaginations. General revelation is all around us; it is every instance of God showing Himself and His character to us through the created order.

Here is an example: from general revelation, we learn that God loves order. Just look at the structure of a honeycomb, or the Fibonacci sequence in the scales of a pinecone. God, as part of His Divine Personality, clearly delights in bringing order—an order that is beautiful and satisfying and useful—to His creation. That's very helpful. But even more helpful is the book of Leviticus, where God reveals how His chosen people are to order their lives and their communities. Here, in the special revelation of the

Bible, we find a whole new level of insight into God's character.

We, as subcreators, are given the gift of participating in general revelation. We, through our day-to-day endeavors in art, science, administration, parenting, gardening, housekeeping, teaching, and so on, have the chance to reveal parts of God's nature to each other. There is no clearer example of this than through the Eucharist. God gives us wheat and grapes, and through the work of human hands, we make that wheat into bread and those grapes into wine. Those things are clearly an improvement, at least in terms of consumption, on wheat and grapes. But God does not stop there. For if we freely offer our creations of bread and wine to Him, in faith, He chooses to use our gifts—the bread and wine that we made!—to reveal Christ to us, to reveal our salvation.

BRINGING *ALL* OUR GIFTS TO THE ALTAR

Let me share a story with you. It starts in my family's kitchen on a Sunday morning. Our church has communion every week, and different people in the congregation take turns baking the bread that we use for Eucharist.

When it is my wife's turn, she gets up a little earlier than usual and mixes water and oil and flour and honey and salt into a simple dough. Then she rolls it out flat and uses the outline of a bowl to carefully cut it into three loaves. She scores each loaf with a cross, which also conveniently makes it easy for the priest to break. On one of those loaves, the one that's going to sit on top, she scores the letters IC XC NIKA, which invokes the ancient Greek phrase meaning *Jesus Christ Conquers.* If our kids wake up before this process is complete, they may get a few bites of uncooked dough or sometimes a little mini loaf of their own.

We take these simple loaves into church, where they sit in the back as people gather in the sanctuary and prepare for worship. And then together, as a congregation, we bless the Lord, and we sing, and we hear the words of holy Scripture read and preached. We declare our faith through the words of the ancient Creed. We pray and confess our sins, and we pass the peace of God to one another. And then, when the time comes, someone from the congregation carries the loaves and the wine up. Then the priest—sometimes me, sometimes one of my brother priests—takes the bread, blesses it, breaks it, and then gives it to the congregation as the body of Christ.

We meet with God in our feast of bread. The bread that was made in my kitchen, out of simple ingredients, is transformed by our act of thanksgiving, by our act of Eucharist, into a special means of grace. The simple gifts of the earth that God has given us—the wheat and the water—are mixed with human creativity as we make a loaf of bread that we offer back to Him. And then He gives it back to us, but He gives it back transformed into something that brings true life.

LIVING EUCHARISTICALLY

This is the calling of the Christian: we are to take what we have been given, our lives, our talents, our bodies, our words, our paints and pencils; whatever medium we use to create art or mode in which we live and work. We are to offer all this up to God in hope and faith that our creation will be transformed into something that offers light for ourselves and for others.

The world needs revelation that only someone who is in Christ can offer. Only Christians—Christian artists, Christian scientists, Christian teachers and parents and workers and volunteers—can perform this particular act of offering *back* to God, the act that gives all our work revelatory power.

As Alexander Schmemann puts it in his book, *For the Life of the World*:

> There must be someone in this world—which rejected God and in this rejection, in this blasphemy, became a chaos of darkness—there must be someone to stand in its center, and to discern, to see it again as full of divine riches, as the cup full of life and joy, as beauty and wisdom, and to thank God for it. This "someone" is Christ, the new Adam who restores that "Eucharistic life" which I, the old Adam, have rejected and lost; who makes me again what I am, and restores the world to me. And if the Church is in Christ, its initial act is always this act of thanksgiving, of returning the world to God.[1]

This is what we are called to do when we become Christians. Christianity is far more than simply going to church once a week. It is a continuous offering of the world back to God, with thanksgiving. And this is no mere sign. As when we do this, we are actually returning the world, which has fallen so far away, back to the God who made it.

A SPECIAL WORD FOR ARTISTS

Clearly this has meaning for all of us, whether we work in the arts or not. But in Christianity, especially American Evangelical Christianity, artists often feel pushed out or undervalued. They feel that their work, unless it is overtly evangelistic, has no place in the Church. So I want to offer a special word to artists here.

Understanding our lives as a continuous Eucharist helps us connect with God as the Trinity—Father, Son, and Holy Spirit—in the creation of art. It is easiest, perhaps, to see how the Holy Spirit participates in artistic creation; He inspires us and shapes our imaginations. But if we think of art as a eucharistic activity—an activity of offering up our gifts to God—we can see how the Son and the Father are also involved in our artistic endeavors.

As Schmemann says, it is the Son who shows us what it looks like for a human to live eucharistically. Jesus came as a man and gave thanks to God for everything in the world. He gave thanks for things that people overlooked. He saw those that the world had seen as outcasts, and said to the Father, "I give You thanks for

these, for the poor, the broken, and the unwise, for the foolish."
He said, "Father, You've given me this cup, that I don't want, of
suffering, and yet still I'll offer this up to You as well."

We see here how Jesus is our model for living a eucharistic
life, and the Father is the one to whom we are offering our art. He
becomes our very first audience for everything that we create.

The idea of God as audience might be terrifying. It's easy to
say, "I can never live up to the expectations of God. How can I
possibly do that?" But if we look at the idea of audience through
this eucharistic lens, then we see that God is active both as
audience and as participant in the creation of our art. He is not
only viewing what we make; He is giving us all the elements
required to make it, and then He is transforming our efforts into
something that can actually offer life.

The bread that my family makes on Sunday morning? It's
just bread. It's good bread, but it's just bread. It can keep my body
alive, but it won't preserve my soul for eternal life. The life the
bread can give me *as bread* is certainly not the life that Jesus talks
about when He said, "I am the bread of the world." It is not the
body of Christ until it is offered to God in the Eucharist.

In the same way, my art is not complete until I offer it to the
Father.

A COMMUNITY OF THANKSGIVING

The Eucharist is first and foremost an activity of the Church. It's something that we gather together to do. I don't bless the loaves at home and *then* bring them into the Body. We come together as a group to offer thanksgiving. God designed things this way on purpose. He gave us an identity as part of the Church, part of God's people, because only in that kind of community can we participate in a eucharistic life. The "offering up" that transforms our creations must happen in community.

Every Christian has a priestly vocation, because every Christian is offering the things of the world up to God, and blessing them, and receiving back something that is good, and beautiful, and complete: something that can offer real life to others. The Church—the physical building, the space, the people, the pastor/leadership—shows us how we are to model our own lives and how we are to offer up the creation to God.

In this way, what we do in church necessarily affects how we interact with the world outside of church. If in church we witness the Eucharist, the transformed gift that comes from a free offering, we can then carry that eucharistic life out into the world. We can practice offering our world back to God and see how He transforms it. We can do this through art, by telling true and beautiful stories that resist false narratives. We can do this through science, by exploring the deepest secrets of the material order and offering our awe to God. We can do it through any true calling that we discern on our lives. When we create, discover, witness, or participate in things that are good, and beautiful, and true, we have a chance to eucharistically guide people into this redemptive story that God is working through us.

In a eucharistic life, there is no stark division between the sacred and the secular. Bread in itself is not sacred, and yet when it's offered up to God, we receive it back as something holy. It is set apart for our life and for our goodness. The same thing is true of our works, our creations, our art. It's not that our art or our work is sacred in itself. That again is a false narrative. But when we offer it up to God with thanksgiving, then it becomes holy.

This act of making things holy is at the core of what it means to live faithfully as a Christian.

UGLINESS THAT LEADS
TO THE GOSPEL

This doesn't mean that Christians must ignore or minimize suffering and tragedy. Quite the contrary; Schmemann says, "Because we have first seen the beauty of the world, we can now see the ugliness, realize what we have lost, understand how our whole life (and not only some 'trespasses') has become sin, and can repent it."

This is a unique gift Christians can offer the world: the ability to *truly* see suffering, to *truly* recognize evil and ugliness, and not to turn away. But that witness, a witness that itself may be marked by ugly words and ugly images, will not lead to hopelessness. For this is an ugliness that points back to beauty, which we see in the gospel, and to the need for redemption through Jesus.

This eucharistic model of creation also has something to say about the quality of our work. If we're offering our work to God, if He is our first audience, we want to offer our best. At the same time, we need not be fearful. The loaves we make for Sunday mornings are not perfect. We offer Him the best that we have, and He receives it and gives us a blessing.

This is consistent throughout the Bible. I think of Jesus looking at the widow offering two small coins and saying she's offering a true gift to God. As an artist, I probably have the widow's budget for what I can offer up to God. But I offer the best that I can, and trust that in Him it is transformed and made into something that is beautiful, and good, and full of life.

YOUR GIFTS TRANSFORMED

I used to do a lot of photography, and my favorite thing about it was how it taught me to see the world. Even when I didn't have a camera with me, if I was thinking through the lens of a camera, I was looking for beauty. Photography taught me to see beauty even when I didn't have my camera with me.

As we practice a eucharistic life, it helps us to prepare for making eucharistic art or doing eucharistic work. It is an amazing and powerful thing to walk around the city, to see people walking by, and to bless them. Not with any announcement of what we are doing, but just say to God, "I see these people. I see this city. And I offer it to You."

We can do this. We can see our world as something that God has given, something good from Him, and we can offer it back to Him, knowing that in Him it can be redeemed. It can be made holy. This changes the way that we see people around us, the way we view challenges and even tragedy. It frees us to say, "I can't see how You're working through this. I can't see the good end in this, but I offer it to You."

So, as we enter into this story, as we enter into this Eucharist life, we receive the things of this earth, we give thanks, we bless them, and we give them back to God. Then we find out that He returns them to us, and now we are people who have true life.

Schmemann says,

> Now in the time in which we can thank God for Christ, we begin to understand that everything is transformed in Christ into its true wonder. In the radiance of his life, the world is not commonplace. The very floor we stand on is a miracle of atoms whizzing about in space. The darkness of sin is clarified, and its burden shouldered. Death is robbed of its finality, trampled down by Christ's death. In a world where everything that seems to be present is immediately past. Everything in Christ is able to participate in eternal present of God.[2]

Look at the world through these eyes, live and work and create with these eyes, and thanks be to God.

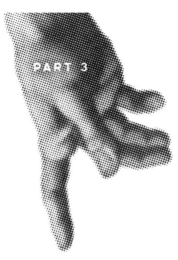

PART 3

God Meets Us in
CREATION

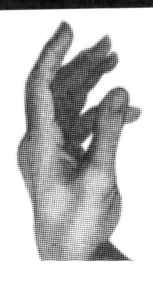

The Call of Creation as Worship

ANTHONY ESOLEN

In this fallen world, we are presented with
both a challenge and an opportunity.
In pursuing beauty and excellence to the
glory of God, we have the opportunity to
learn from the great creators of the past,
our partners in subcreation. But the challenge
in doing so is that we cannot learn directly
from them—the passing on of training and
traditions has partially been lost. How can
we accept the calling of the Creator and
learn the stewardship that comes with it?

When the poet John Milton imagined Adam and Eve, sinless, in the garden of Eden, it was as the king and queen of the world, still learning about the creatures around them, and *tending* the earth. On the first evening when we meet them, Adam draws attention to their labor, which for them is a delight, not a sore necessity. He and Eve have enjoyed their innocent dinner, which

includes conversation about the stars, and talk of when they first
met, and, of course, the kisses of love. But the time for their sleep
draws near, says Adam, and so they must take their rest, to repair
their bodies and their minds for the work on the next day:

> Man hath his daily work of body or mind
> Appointed, which declares his dignity,
> And the regard of heaven on all his ways;
> While other animals unactive range,
> And of their doings God takes no account.

That is, God does not reckon the value of what each animal
does, because although the animals do things, they do not *take
action:* God does not stand before them as a judge well-pleased
with their selections, their arrangements, the intelligent changes
they bring to the world He has given them. Adam implies that God
does take account of what he and Eve do, as a loving and generous
father appreciates the work, the gift, that a good son gives him.

But we must not think of God as a taskmaster. Before their
fall into sin, the work that Adam and Eve do is always a form
of art. God has not simply given them a beautiful garden. He
has given them a garden they are to make more beautiful and
commodious for themselves. They are to leave, so to speak, the
impress of their fingers and their persons on all they touch. It is
as if God has freely given them the authority and the encourage-
ment to be the gods of their new world, to "have dominion," as
the sacred author puts it, over all the creatures in it.

Now, that does not mean that Adam and Eve create. God

alone creates: the Hebrew verb *bara'* is used, in Scripture, exclusively with God as the subject. Nothing so exalted and exclusive did the pagans roundabout them believe about their rabble of gods. We might say that pagans, ancient and modern both, reduce God to Mr. Zeus, the politician, or Mr. Apollo, the singer and player on the lute; in general, to large and often treacherous and threatening versions of themselves. The satyr Marsyas *can* challenge Apollo to a music contest, and though it is presumptuous of him to do so, and though he is bound to lose, and he is flayed alive for his punishment, the contest is, to the Greek mind, conceivable. Such a thing is inconceivable to the Hebrew mind, in whose sacred poetry there is as little anthropomorphism as is possible for human beings to say anything at all about God without collapsing into complete abstraction.

That is because, among the Hebrews, the relationship is the reverse: the God they are not permitted to reduce to carven imagery has made man in *His* ineffable and indescribable image and likeness. And we have spent three thousand years meditating upon what that means. The partial answer that we in this book have given is that man is meant by his Creator to be a maker, to give of himself lovingly in art that reflects the beauty, the goodness, and the truth of the world that God has given him. God is not, like the imaginary Apollo, jealous of his art.

So it is that Milton shows Adam and Eve to be artists in fact. With care and intelligence and love, under no specific command of God or oversight by the angels, they give new form to created things. Again, Adam speaks to Eve, and reveals to us what their innocent work is all about:

> Tomorrow ere fresh morning streak the east
> With first approach of light, we must be risen,
> And at our pleasant labor, to reform
> Yon flowery arbors, yonder alleys green,
> Our walk at noon, with branches overgrown,
> That mock our scant manuring, and require
> More hands than ours to lop their wanton growth;
> Those blossoms also, and those dropping gums,
> That lie bestrown unsightly and unsmooth,
> Ask riddance, if we mean to tread with ease;
> Meanwhile, as Nature wills, night bids us rest.

It is to make the garden a garden for man: with arbors and
alleys and clearings and shady recesses; not a violation of nature,
but a fulfillment. God gives with a free hand, for, as Milton
describes it, "Nature boon" has poured forth flowers "profuse
on hill and dale and plain," and even the caves are overhung
with plenty, where "the mantling vine / Lays forth her purple
grape, and gently creeps / Luxuriant." That means that Adam
and Eve enjoy both abundant matter for their art, and abundant
opportunity to express it, mainly by a kind of circumscription, by
setting boundaries. They clear away paths for their convenience.
They prune back the bounty of the garden, just as, we may say,
they dress their own inner passions, not so that the passions will
be damp and dull, but that they may flow all the more mightily
in the right direction. Why, their very art, as Eve will say on the

fateful morning when the two, for the first time, work separately, gives bountiful nature more and not less impetus to grow:

> Till more hands
> Aid us, the work under our labor grows,
> Luxurious by restraint; what we by day
> Lop overgrown, or prune, or prop, or bind,
> One night or two with wanton growth derides
> Tending to wild.

Such art does not put nature under suspicion. It is the check, the limitation, that fosters, improves, channels, blesses, even brings into being that which was before was not. In this way too it reflects the action of the Creator, as Milton describes it when the Word of God, the coeternal Son through whom all things were made, places limits upon the welter of unformed matter first created:

> He took the golden Compasses, prepared
> In God's eternal store, to circumscribe
> This universe, and all created things:
> One foot he centered, and the other turned
> Round through the vast profundity obscure,
> And said, "Thus far extend, thus far thy bounds,
> This be thy just circumference, O World."

Milton is echoing the ringing words of God, when He shuts the sea within its doors: "Thus far shall you come, and no farther, and here shall your proud waves be stayed" (Job 38:11).

In our time we have, I believe, bought a notion of art that

violates art's relationship to God's created nature, and that is very
quickly destructive of art itself. "True wit is nature to advantage
dressed," says Alexander Pope, but we have assumed rather the
contrary, that there is no such thing as human nature, and that it
is the function of the artist to transgress all boundaries, and to be
"original." And thus have we flooded the world with originality,
dreary and incoherent and predictably unpredictable, slavish to
mass entertainment and mass media, and gnostic or nihilist in
the vacuity that should be its soul. What is a work of art? Said
one feminist, pretending to possess the power though not the
goodness or the love of God, "It's a work of art if I say it is." We do
not get Michelangelo that way, or Bach, or Dante.

   That sort of thing is, in fact, demonic. Satan attempts it when
he insists to Beelzebub, as those two fallen angels first survey the
terrible place that is now their dwelling, that naming need have
nothing to do with external reality: "The mind is its own place,
and in itself / Can make a Heaven of Hell, a Hell of Heaven." It is
the evil mimic or perversion of what Adam does when he names
the beasts, by the generous grant of God. Adam names them by
recognizing what in them is most proper to them, most characteristic, which, because all things have been created by God as good,
must also be what is best and most beautiful. If God graciously
submits to His creature Adam so that "whatever the man called
every living creature, that was its name" (Genesis 2:19), Adam, in
the naming, graciously submits to the nature of the living thing
as made by God. That remains true, we see, even after the fall, as
we hear Adam name his wife Eve, Hebrew *Chawwah,* "because

she was the mother of all living" (3:20), punning on the verb *chawah, to live.* Then Eve names her firstborn son, Cain, punning on the verb *qanah, to get,* saying, "I have gotten a man with the help of the Lord" (4:1).

I wish to make two points here. If we are speaking of *subcreation,* to cite the wonderful and profoundly suggestive term that Tolkien has bequeathed to us, and if we are to engage in it most truly and profitably, we must respect both parts of the word, that is, the prefix and the root. We must respect *creation,* that is, the nature of things that we have not made, by loving them and taking our lead from them, allowing ourselves, as Bernadette Waterman Ward has said, considering the poet Gerard Manley Hopkins, to be moved by their "inscape," their inner essence, their being-themselves. That means that we receive them as gifts, not as mere stuff to be ground to powder in an industrial machine, or in the grinding gears of human egotism. We respect *their* boundaries. At the same time, we must keep in mind that we come nearest to God's creative act when we acknowledge God Himself as the source of man's yearning toward art, and the highest object of that art. We thank God for *our* boundaries, and in our thanks, which is our free gift, we participate most heartily in God's gratuitous action. The artist, insofar as he is a fully human being, looks to God.

God inspires, in both meanings of the word: it is ultimately His Spirit that breathes in the true artist, whether the artist knows it or not, or whether he uses that inspiration for the best; and in our contemplation of God, in our thanks and our praise, we are moved to want to make—to sing, as David and Asaph and the sons of Korah did; to build what is glorious and beautiful, as did the craftsmen under the direction of Moses. "See," says Moses to the sons of Israel,

> The Lord has called by name Bezalel the son of Uri, son of Hur, of the tribe of Judah; and he has filled him with the Spirit of God, with ability, with intelligence, with knowledge, and all craftsmanship, to devise artistic designs, to work in gold and silver and bronze, in cutting stones for setting, and in carving wood, for work in every skilled craft" (Exodus 35:30–32).

Bezalel and Oholiab not only know what to do, in "every sort of work done by a craftsman or by a designer or by an embroiderer in blue and purple and scarlet stuff and fine twined linen" (v. 35), but they can also teach the art, and direct the work of craftsmen beneath them. For they are not the only artists among the people, but they are joined by "every able man in whose mind the Lord had put ability, every one whose heart stirred him up to come to do the work" (36:2).

What the text implies, of course, is that not everyone will have been granted the skill to do the work that Bezalel and Oholiab direct. Still, the impulse is universal to man. Even those who cannot make, because the understanding is not in their hands, can, by their grateful beholding and receiving, participate in the work of art in the fullest sense, because the work is for God, is man's gift to God that elevates man in the giving, as all true gifts do. We can imagine the full heart of the psalmist, who sings out, "I rejoiced when I heard them say, Let us go up to the house of the Lord" (Psalm 122:1). The Chronicler places us on the scene when Solomon's temple is complete, and the Ark of the Covenant is brought within. So many arts are on full display, carpentry, masonry, sculpture in wood and in gold and silver, toolmaking, and perhaps the purest of all the arts, the music of the human voice in song:

> And when the priests came out of the Holy Place . . . and all the Levitical singers, Asaph, Heman, and Jeduthun, their sons and kinsmen, arrayed in fine linen, with cymbals, harps, and lyres, stood east of the altar with a hundred and twenty priests who were trumpeters; and it was the duty of the trumpeters and singers to make themselves heard in unison in praise and thanksgiving to the Lord, and when the song was raised, with trumpets and cymbals and other musical instruments, in praise to the Lord, 'For he is good, for his mercy endures forever,' the house, the house of the Lord, was filled with a cloud, so that the priests could not stand to minister because of the cloud; for the glory of the Lord filled the house of God" (2 Chronicles 5:11–14).

The smallest child whose heart is taken up by the grandeur and the song joins in the work of the artist.

Now then, how do we praise God best? The Lord has said that he who humbles himself shall be exalted, and that is true of the arts also. Milton's Adam and Eve are, before the fall, fine

and noble artists *because* they submit, they open themselves
up to the goodness of being. They compose their own prayers,
and their minds are so clear and sharp, that they sing a kind of
spontaneous poetry. So they wake up in the morning, and before
they take up a single garden task, they turn to God:

> Lowly they bowed adoring, and began
> Their orisons, each morning duly paid
> In various style, for neither various style
> Nor holy rapture wanted they to praise
> Their Maker, in fit strains pronounced or sung
> Unmeditated, such prompt eloquence
> Flowed from their lips, in prose, or numerous verse,
> More tunable than needed lute or harp
> To add more sweetness.

The prayer that follows parallels Psalm 148, and its most
notable feature is its structure, its fine repetitions, as the happy
couple turn from heaven to earth and to all the creatures on
earth in due order, from the highest to the lowest, to give praise to
God. That they do not have to meditate upon it, sweating over a
sheet of paper and scribbling out one word after another, reveals
something about them in particular, and not about the sort of
art that we, whose minds are not so clear and sharp and whose
hearts are not sinless and true, must condescend to compose.

To be a poet now, or someone who might hope to compose
a single measure of music worthy of Bach, or to paint a single
leaf, as Tolkien's Niggle of happy memory does, that is somehow

in the same cathedral with Michelangelo, we must respect the *matter* of our art, the created or man-made stuff. It is not infinitely malleable to our will: we are not God. But more—in the very limitation that it sets upon us, it invites us to work with it in limitation, in a kind of dance of boundaries, with the artist submitting to the characteristics of the matter, and the matter submitting to the form the artist imposes upon it. And it is just here that I wish to sound a warning to my fellow Christians, or a call to action, depending upon how one wishes to take it.

Moses did not assume that anybody and everybody was a goldsmith or a fine weaver, and Solomon went far afield, all the way to Tyre, to find Huramabi, a Danite who, as the king of Tyre says, was "trained to work in gold, silver, bronze, iron, stone, and wood, and in purple, blue, and crimson fabrics and fine linen, and to do all sorts of engraving and execute any design that may be assigned him" (2 Chronicles 2:14). Where do we go to find Huramabi now?

It is simply not true that artistic knowledge is simply absorbed into a general fund for man to draw upon when he wills. Hand must be trained by hand. It is not simply the case that no one *has* sculpted as Michelangelo did. No one can; no one can even do a fair imitation, because the art, all the habits of mind and eye and hand, the knowledge of different kinds of marble, the way to feel what is, so to speak, latent within a block of stone, has not been passed on. We do not now build Chartres Cathedral, not merely because we are not inspired to do so, but because the thousands of mainly nameless skills and points of knowledge have been lost.

Even in poetry—which one may learn without a hand guiding a hand, but merely with a mind and an ear, a voice and an inner eye, willing to learn from the poet we are reading—I think there are countless skills we have lost. I "hear" as much when I read poetry by well-meaning Christians attempting to write in a traditional meter, and it becomes clear to me that they do not know the stuff, the matter of the art; they do not know what that meter is and what it can do, given the formal and phonological properties of English. But I also see it when I note that many a thing that poets in the not very distant past used to do are no longer done in verse at all, such as to tell a complex story, to create characters revealing themselves in a dramatic situation by what they do and say, or—dare I mention it—to sing, to sing in a song whose structure might inspire a Bach to arrange it and robe it in splendor, as he did with the poetic text *Jesu, Meine Freude.*

Here, as so often, Christians are presented with both a challenge and an opportunity. The fact is, *only* people who believe as we do will now be willing to be subcreators, giving honor to the Creator and to the natures He has created, and extending that honor also to works of artistic genius that subcreators before us have wrought. Our secular fellows have made it a point of pride—and, I think, it illustrates bad faith, cowardice, folly, and incompetence—*not to learn from their fathers, not to learn from masters of the art.* Whether they might, with a good will, be led to learn from Bach without Bach's indwelling faith, I do not know. I do know, because I observe what they have done and I listen to what they say, that they have no intention of making the attempt.

For modernism is a kind of murdering of the father. Like the prodigal in the parable of Jesus, the modernist quickly squanders his heritage, and he is now reduced to feeding slops to swine, but, unlike the prodigal, he pronounces it good, and says that everybody has always been a feeder of swine, or a swine indeed. He is an author of dystopias, but with no sane and sweet homeland he loves by contrast. It is all orc, and no Shire.

We of all people must not be that way. But that will require of us a great deal of humility and patience. As artists, we must recognize how much we have lost, and how much we must recover—far more than we suppose—and the more we recover, the more we will see that is yet to be recovered. We must not fool ourselves. Take a savage who has never seen a wheel and put him on the runway of an airport. That is what we are by comparison with Milton. If I exaggerate the distance, I do not exaggerate the urgency and the need, once again, to undergo the slow process of learning and respecting the matter of the art we choose to practice. The boy Michelangelo had to do his apprenticeship in the studio of Ghirlandaio, learning how to grind the stuff of paints with a mortar and pestle. It is time to mix our hands into the stuff. To farm three feet square of soil in a perfect way, as Tolkien once said it was his ambition to do, you must get your hands dirty in the earth; you must know seeds, and water, and air, and sunlight, and the food that the plants you choose like or do not like. You cannot do it by theory, or by all the good and holy intentions in the world. Everyone else is slovenly and unwilling to learn. Let us not be so!

ENDNOTES

FRONT MATTER

1 N. T. Wright, *Ask NT Wright Anything* podcast, episode 142 "Q&A on New Creation & Salvation," aired Oct. 21, 2022.

PROLOGUE

1 Dorothy L. Sayers, *Letters to a Diminished Church: Passionate Arguments for the Relevance of Christian Doctrine* (Nashville, TN: Thomas Nelson, 2004), 41.

2 Ibid., 25.

3 Ibid., qtd. on 31.

4 Ibid., 20–21.

5 *They Stand Together: The Letters of C. S. Lewis to Arthur Greeves, 1914–1963*, ed. Walter Hooper (New York: Macmillan, 1979), 427.

CHAPTER 1

1 J. R. R. Tolkien, *Tales from the Perilous Realm* (Boston: Houghton, Mifflin, Harcourt, 2008), 257–258.

2 Alexander Schmemann, *Of Water and the Spirit: A Liturgical Study of Baptism* (Crestwood, NY: St. Vladimir's Seminary Press, 1974), 49.

CHAPTER 2

1 Alexander Schmemann, *Church, World, Mission* (Crestwood, NY: St. Vladimir's Seminary Press, 1979), 220.

2 St. Basil the Great, *On the Human Condition*, Nonna Verna Harrison, trans. (Crestwood, NY: St. Vladimir's Seminary Press, 2005), 51.

3 Gerald L. Schroeder, *The Science of God: The Convergence of Scientific and Biblical Wisdom* (New York: The Free Press, 1997), 177.

4 St. Basil, 32.

CHAPTER 3

1 Carlo Rovelli, *The Order of Time: Seven Brief Lessons on Physics*, Erica Segre, Simon Carnell, trans. (New York: Riverhead, 2018), 57.

2 Ecclesiastes 3:2–4.

3 Ibid., 128.

4 Ibid., 45.

5 Ibid., 24.

6 Ibid., 33.

7 Ibid., 125.

8 Ibid., 123.

9 C. S. Lewis, *Letters to Malcolm: Chiefly on Prayer* (Estate of C. S. Lewis, 1963, 1964), 110.

10 C. S. Lewis, *The Great Divorce* (New York: HarperCollins, 1946; renewed 1973), 69.

CHAPTER 4

1 The story is available online at https://wp.lps.org/mpayant/files/2010/08/LEAF-BY-NIGGLE.pdf.

2 Summa Theologiae, I.93.1.

3 Ibid., I.93.1.

4 Ibid., I.45.5.

5 See J. R. R. Tolkien, *Tolkien on Fairy-Stories*, Verlyn Flieger, Douglas A. Anderson, eds. (London: HarperCollins, 2014).

6 Tolkien is in fact dependent on Thomas. See Jonathan McIntosh, *The Imperishable Flame: Tolkien, Thomas, and the Metaphysics of Faerie* (Brooklyn, NY: Angelico Press, 2017).

7 Robert Miner, *Truth in the Making: Creative Knowledge in Theology and Philosophy* (London: Routledge, 2013), 9.

8 This illustration and the argument of the following paragraphs draws on Walker Percy, *Symbol and Existence: A Study in Meaning: Explorations in Human Nature* (Macon, GA: Mercer University Press, 2019).

9   My reading has been guided by J. Samuel Hammond, "Creation and Sub-creation in Leaf by Niggle," *Inklings Forever*, vol. 7 (2020), https://pillars.taylor.edu/inklings_forever/vol7/iss1/7/

CHAPTER 5

1   Josef Pieper, *Happiness & Contemplation*, Richard and Clara Winston, trans. (South Bend, IN: St. Augustine's Press, 1998), 26.
2   See page xviii.
3   William Edgar, *Created and Creating: A Biblical Theology of Culture* (Downers Grove, IL: InterVarsity Press, 2017), 189.
4   Pieper, *Happiness & Contemplation*, 84, 85.
5   Flannery O'Connor, *A Prayer Journal* (New York: Farrar, Straus and Giroux, 2013), 3.
6   Pieper, 26.
7   Martin Schleske, *The Sound of Life's Unspeakable Beauty*, Janet Gesme, trans. (Grand Rapids, MI: Eerdmans, 2020), 181.
8   Ted Prescott, in private communication with the author, May 15, 2022.
9   Schleske, *Unspeakable Beauty*, 181.
10   Leslie Anne Bustard, *The Goodness of the Lord in the Land of the Living: Selected Poems by Leslie Anne Bustard* (Baltimore, MD: Square Halo Books, 2023), 46.
11   Luke LeDuc, "Best Use of the Time," Wheatland Presbyterian Church, May 8, 2022, Lancaster, PA.

CHAPTER 6

1   See C. S. Lewis, *Bluspels and Flalansferes: A Semantic Nightmare, Selected Literary Essays*, ed. Walter Hooper (Cambridge: Cambridge University Press, 1969).
2   See David Hicks, *Norms and Nobility: A Treatise on Education* (New York: Prager, 1981).
3   Ibid.
4   See J. R. R. Tolkien, *On Fairy-stories*, Verlyn

Flieger, Douglas A. Anderson, eds. (New York: HarperCollins, 2014).

CHAPTER 7

1   Found at https://www.etymonline.com/word/colony; last accessed on 9/19/2022.
2   Fyodor Dostoevsky, *The Brothers Karamazov*, trans. by Constance Garnett (New York: The Lowell Press, 1930); accessed via Project Gutenberg: https://www.gutenberg.org/files/28054/28054-h/28054-h.htm.
3   Norman Wirzba, *This Sacred Life: Humanity's Place in a Wounded World* (Cambridge, England: Cambridge University Press, 2021), xix.
4   Scripture references are taken from the English Standard Version.
5   Acts 17:28.
6   Ethan Blake, "Could the Ancient Jewish Practice of Shmita Be a New Tool for Sustainable Ag?" *Civil Eats* (March 28, 2019).
7   See Tim Ingold, *Being Alive: Essays on Movement, Knowledge and Description* (New York: Routledge, 2011). Norman Wirzba also has a chapter on Ingold's meshwork theory in *This Sacred Life*.
8   Wendell Berry, "A Native Hill," in *The World-Ending Fire* (New York: Penguin, 2018), 23.
9   Luke 12:24.
10   J. R. R. Tolkien, *The Lord of the Rings: The Fellowship of the Ring*, 120.
11   Ibid.
12   Saint Augustine, *Confessions*, trans. by R. S. Pine-Coffin (New York: Penguin, 2002), 226.
13   Psalm 19:1.
14   George MacDonald, *Discovering the Character of God* (New York: Rosetta Books, 2018); ebook.
15   Dostoevsky, Project Gutenberg.

CHAPTER 8

1   T. S. Eliot, *The Complete Poems and Plays 1909–1950* (New York: Harcourt, Brace, Jovanovich, 1971), 149.

2   Neil Douglas-Klotz, *Prayers of the Cosmos: Meditations on the Aramaic Words of Jesus* (New York, NY: Harper One, 2009), 16.

CHAPTER 9

1   "The lack of a deliberate connection between the writer and his readers may be one of the factors that makes *The Silmarillion* demanding to read, challenging to connect with, and less popular than *The Lord of the Rings*. I suggest that *The Lord of the Rings* might have been much more like *The Silmarillion* in structure and style if it had not been so strongly influenced by the 'humanizing' effect of the Inklings." Diana Pavlac Glyer, *The Company They Keep: C. S. Lewis and J. R. R. Tolkien as Writers in Community* (Kent, OH: Kent State Univ. Press, 2008), 65.

2   J.R.R. Tolkien, *Tree and Leaf: Including the Poem Mythopoeia* (Boston: Houghton Mifflin, 1989), 65.

3   Christie Purifoy, *Roots and Sky: A Journey Home in Four Seasons* (Grand Rapids, MI: Revell, 2016), 189.

4   Roger Lundin quoting Robert Jensen: "Instead of thinking of time as an extension of finite consciousness, Jensen suggests, we should consider its 'stretching out' to be a matter of its being contained within the 'infinite enveloping consciousness' of God. We are players and participants, that is, in a drama that takes place 'within the divine life.'" In Roger Lundin, *Beginning with the Word: Modern Literature and the Question of Belief* (Grand Rapids, MI: Baker Academic, 2014), 129.

5   Paraphrase of Psalm 8.

6   Thomas Howard, *Chance or the Dance: A Critique of Modern Secularism* (San Francisco: Ignatius Press, 2001), 120, 126.

7   I'm paraphrasing Tolkien, who in his essay *On Fairy-stories*, points out that "It is man who is, in contrast to fairies, supernatural." *On Fairy-stories* (London: HarperCollins, 2014), 10.

8   Transcribed from the introductory sequence of *"Jim Henson's The Storyteller,"* a television series that ran 1987–1988. This was in the intro sequence.

9   Roger Lundin did a great job of tracing the development of structuralism, which is naturalism working itself into language and meaning, in his book *Beginning with the Word*.

10 From Ned Bustard, Melody Green, eds., foreword by Devin Brown, *J. R. R. Tolkien and the Arts: A Theology of Subcreation* (Baltimore, MD: Square Halo Books, 2021), 63. The extract comes from my essay in the collection which includes a quote ("which means to read or understand into a thing, to penetrate the interior quality of a thing with one's mind") originally from David L. Schindler, *Love and the Postmodern Predicament: Rediscovering the Real in Beauty, Goodness, and Truth* (Eugene, OR: Cascade Books, 2018), 77–78.

11 Josef Pieper, *Only the Lover Sings: Art and Contemplation* (San Francisco: Ignatius Press, 1990), 35.

12 The practical intellect is most interested in the action of making something out of what it discovers, as opposed to the speculative intellect, which is most interested in knowing for knowing's own sake.

13 Jacques Maritain, *Art and Scholasticism* (Providence, RI: Cluny Media, 2020), 15.

14 Andy Crouch, *Culture Making: Recovering Our Creative Calling* (Downers Grove, IL: Intervarsity Press, 2013), 10.

15 The concept of mystery in the New Testament is almost the opposite of our common connotation of something closed or hidden. Rather, it is something being opened and made available. Jesus is inviting us into mystery, with deeper and deeper participation being made ever more available to us.

16 Lundin, 204.

17 Christianity teaches that word and thing bear a true correspondence in reality that must be honored. In contrast, Structuralism paves the way for personal advantage to become the only qualifier for naming, since for "structuralism, as Saussure defines it, to have the word always means not to have the thing because by its nature the presence of the sign implies the absence of the concept or reality to which it refers." Lundin, 51.

18 Esther Lightcap Meek's writings have been a huge help to me in this regard. She argues that knowing depends on loving. Similarly, Hans Urs von Balthasar orders the transcendentals with beauty first, goodness second, and truth last. This suggests that beauty invites us to pursue a right, loving relationship with any object (goodness) if we're to arrive finally at the truth.

19 Ken Myers, Mars Hill Audio Journal, Vol 142; https://marshillaudio.org (last accessed Aug. 8, 2022).

20 Alexander Schmemann and Paul Kachur, *The Eucharist: Sacrament of the Kingdom* (Crestwood, NY: St. Vladimir's Seminary Press, 1987), 38.

21 Romans 1:20.

22 That's why the Eucharist affects anamnesis: the healing and negation of amnesia; dis-membered humanity is re-membered to her true name and family as God's beloved bride. The Eucharist is a mystical (and marital) point of union; to take the consecrated elements into ourselves is to say "Amen" to the God who, through Christ, has opened the way for us to be received into Himself. It is to say yes to a proposal that locates us in a meaningful sequence of loving memory, settling us within God's mighty acts (in the past), and anchoring us in a blessed hope (for the future).

23 Tolkien assures us in his essay "On Fairy-stories" that "Each leaf … is a unique embodiment of the pattern, and for some this very year may be *the* embodiment, the first ever seen and recognized, though oaks have put forth leaves for countless generations of men." Tolkien, 52.

24 Gerald Manley Hopkins, "Pied Beauty," https://www.poetryfoundation.org/poems/44399/pied-beauty (last accessed Aug. 20, 2022).

25 "For man, to 'be' means to 'be on the way'—he cannot be in any other form; man is intrinsically a pilgrim." Pieper, *Only the Lover Sings*, 42.

26 J. R. R. Tolkien, *The Silmarillion* (Boston: George Allen & Unwin, 1977), 43–44.

27 God's is an ordered creation, our rebellion insubordinate—a rejection of that order. Ministers are *ordained*, which is to say, restored to a proper relation within God's order of things as ones who might ad*minister* that lost order. Subcreation, in a manner of speaking, is part of coming home to our rightful place in the order of things. To reject inordinate creation and submit to our role as *sub*creators, then, is to accept a kind of natural ordination to serve a priestly role as

caretakers and collaborators in, under, and with our Creator as restorers of *shalom*: right order (right relationships) among all things.

28 Interestingly, magic tricks depend on an observer entirely underestimating the amount of construct that's gone into achieving a deception. Most of us are unaware of the degree to which a complex deceptive construct has, by now, been taken for granted as objective reality. For us, the trick is reversed: the enchantment has made the world appear less enchanted.

29 Lundin writes in *Beginning with the Word*, "*Semeia* in the New Testament is the clear sense that a sign can never be understood on its own in isolation from what it serves, which is the larger account of God's power and glory especially as they are embodied in the person and work of Jesus Christ" (166).

30 C. S. Lewis, *The Last Battle, the Chronicles of Narnia* (New York: HarperCollins, 1994), 211.

31 David F. Ford, *The Drama of Living: Becoming Wise in the Spirit* (Grand Rapids, MI: Brazos Press, 2014), 186.

32 Our true nature is the Imago Dei, but sin has supplanted the natural with an un-nature. This has gone on so long now that this un-nature feels more natural to us than our true nature.

33 C. S. Lewis, *Till We Have Faces: A Myth Retold* (Boston: Harcourt, 2012), 294.

34 From Tolkien's poem *Mythopoeia*, published in *Tree and Leaf*.

35 A favorite usage of Tolkien's, and of course, the fitting word. According to etymonline. com, "Mar comes from "Middle English merren 'to deface, disfigure; impair in form or substance' (early 13c.), from Old English merran (Anglian), *mierran* (West Saxon) 'to waste, spoil,' from Proto-Germanic *marzjan* (source also of Old Frisian *meria*, Old High German *marren* 'to hinder, obstruct,' Gothic *marzjan* 'to hinder, offend'), from PIE root *mers*—'to trouble, confuse'." (Last accessed at https://www.etymonline.com/search?q=mar&ref=searchbar_searchhint on 11/29/2022.)

36 Is it possible that this ever-expanding universe *is* the storehouse of materials from that postponed shop class? Might we pick up where we left off, rejoining our Master as He teaches students, now redeemed and trustworthy, to work alongside Him with the full spectrum of materiality—from atoms to galaxies and beyond?

37 Tolkien, *Mythopoeia*.

38 2 Peter 1:4.

39 1 Corinthians 2:9.

CHAPTER 10

1 Alexander Schmemann, *For the Life of the World: Sacraments and Orthodoxy* (Crestwood, NY: St. Vladimir's Seminary Press, 1998), 60–61.

2 Ibid., 62.

About the Editors

JANE CLARK SCHARL is a poet and critic. Her poetry has appeared in many American and European outlets, including the BBC, *The Hudson Review, The New Ohio Review, The American Journal of Poetry, The Lamp, Measure Review,* and others. Her criticism has appeared in *Dappled Things, Fare Forward, Plough Quarterly,* and others. She just published *Sonnez Les Matines, a Verse Play* (Belmont, NC: Wiseblood Books 2023). She is a Senior Editor at *The European Conservative.*

BRIAN BROWN is the founder and Executive Director of the Anselm Society, an organization dedicated to a renaissance of the Christian imagination. He also serves as Vice President of Programs for the Colson Center. He studied political theory at Princeton University and political theology at the John Jay Institute, and has consulted as a scholar, researcher, and business strategist with over a hundred spiritual formation and educational institutions. He has a thoroughly intemperate fascination with mythology and the novels of Jane Austen. He lives in Colorado with his wife and two children.

About the Contributors

HANS BOERSMA is the Saint Benedict Servants of Christ Professor in Ascetical Theology at Nashotah House Theological Seminary. He holds a PhD in historical theology from the University of Utrecht, and is an ordained priest in the Anglican Church in North America. Hans's latest book is *Pierced by Love: Divine Reading with the Christian Tradition* (Lexham, 2023). He is known especially for *Heavenly Participation: The Weaving of a Sacramental Tapestry* (Eerdmans, 2011). Hans and his wife, Linda, have five children and fifteen grandchildren.

BRIAN BROWN is the founder and Executive Director of the Anselm Society, an organization dedicated to a renaissance of the Christian imagination. He also serves as Vice President of Programs for the Colson Center. He studied political theory at Princeton University and political theology at the John Jay Institute, and has consulted as a scholar, researcher, and business strategist with over a hundred spiritual formation and educational institutions. He has a thoroughly intemperate fascination with mythology and the novels of Jane Austen. He lives in Colorado with his wife and two children.

PAUL BUCKLEY is a graduate of Westminster Theological Seminary in Philadelphia. He teaches for the

Theopolis Institute in Birmingham, Alabama. He is a former assistant religion editor for *The Dallas Morning News* and for thirteen years was the director of worship at Grace Presbyterian Church in Ocala, Florida, and now serves in Texas at the Colleyville Presbyterian Church.

LESLIE BUSTARD is the author of *The Goodness of the Lord in the Land of the Living: Selected Poems of Leslie Bustard* and co-editor of *Wild Things and Castles in the Sky: A Guide to Choosing the Best Books for Children.* As Vice President of Square Halo Books, she organizes its conferences and hosts the podcast *The Square Halo.* Leslie writes for the *Cultivating Project, Black Barn Online,* and *Story Warren.* She and her husband, Ned, enjoy spending time with their three daughters as well as serving their church family and encouraging art-making communities.

MATTHEW CLARK is a singer/songwriter and storyteller from Mississippi. His several full-length albums include a Bible walk-through called "Bright Came the Word from His Mouth" and "Beautiful Secret Life," songs highlighting, in George Herbert's phrase, "heaven in ordinary." Matthew's current project is "The Well Trilogy": three full-length album/ book combos releasing over three years. He also hosts a weekly podcast, *One Thousand Words—Stories on the Way.*

ANTHONY ESOLEN is a professor of humanities and Writer-in-Residence at Magdalen College, in Warner, NH. He has written or translated twenty-eight books on literature, sacred music, theology, education, and marriage, including a three-volume edition of Dante's *Divine Comedy* (Modern Library), and his own book-length poetic work centering on the life of Christ: *The Hundred-fold: Songs for the Lord* (Ignatius). He and his wife, Debra, publish a web-magazine, Word and Song, devoted to poetry, hymns, classic films, popular songs, and the quirks of our English language.

PETER J. LEITHART is President of Theopolis Institute and serves as Teacher at Trinity Presbyterian Church in Birmingham. His received his PhD at the University of Cambridge in England. He is the author of many books and articles, including *On Earth as in Heaven* (Lexham) and a book on God the Creator forthcoming from IVP. He writes a biweekly column at FirstThings.com. He and his wife, Noel, have ten children and fifteen grandchildren.

MARILYN MCENTYRE'S books include *Caring for Words in a Culture of Lies* (2021) and *Speaking Peace in a Climate of Conflict* (2020). Her book *What's in a Phrase? Pausing Where Scripture Gives You Pause* won the 2015 *Christianity Today* book award in spirituality. Her deepest interests lie in connections between spirituality, language, healing earth and each other. She leads retreats and workshops and teaches for Western Seminary, Westmont College, and New College Berkeley. More at *marilynmcentyre.com*.

GRACE OLMSTEAD, a writer who focuses on agriculture, community, and place, is the author of *Uprooted: Recovering the Legacy of the Places We've Left Behind* (2021). Her writing has been published in *The New York Times,* the *Washington Post,*

National Review, the *Wall Street Journal,* and *Christianity Today.* A native of rural Idaho, she lives outside of Washington, DC, with her husband and three children.

JEROMIE RAND is the rector at Christ Our Hope Anglican Church in Fort Collins, Colorado. He enjoys stories of all sorts—he is never far from a book—and sees part of his calling as a pastor to be a holy storyteller, telling over and over again the story of what God has done for us in Christ and how this good news changes everything.

JANE CLARK SCHARL is a poet and critic. Her poetry has appeared in many American and European outlets, including the BBC, *The Hudson Review, The New Ohio Review, The American Journal of Poetry, The Lamp, Measure Review,* and others. Her criticism has appeared in *Dappled Things, Fare Forward, Plough Quarterly,* and others. She just published *Sonnez Les Matines, a Verse Play* (Belmont, NC: Wiseblood Books 2023). She is a Senior Editor at *The European Conservative.*

HEIDI WHITE is a classical educator, podcaster, consultant, and author. She teaches Humanities at St. Hild School in Colorado Springs and is the author of the forthcoming *The Divided Soul: Reuniting Duty and Desire in Literature and Life.* She is a contributing author, speaker, consultant, and Atrium instructor at the Circe Institute and a weekly contributor on the Close Reads Podcast Network. She serves on the Board of Directors of The Anselm. She lives in Black Forest, Colorado, with her husband and children.

JESSICA HOOTEN WILSON is the inaugural
Visiting Scholar of Liberal Arts at Pepperdine. She is the author
of several books, recently *The Scandal of Holiness: Renewing Your
Imagination in the Company of Literary Saints*. Her book *Giving
the Devil His Due: Demonic Authority in the Fiction of Flannery
O'Connor and Fyodor Dostoevsky* received a 2018 *Christianity Today*
book of the year in arts and culture award. Other awards include
a Fulbright Fellowship, an NEH to study Dante in Florence, and a
Biola University sabbatical fellowship funded by the John Templeton Foundation. She is a Senior Fellow at the Trinity Forum.

Acknowledgments

In creating this book, we are indebted to more people than we
have space to thank: the Arts Guild of the Anselm Society for
helping provide the questions, the Society's members whose
gifts funded the project, the churches that have supported and
partnered with the Society for years, and of course the incredible
writers who contributed to the book. But we are especially
grateful to Heidi White, Christina Brown, and Amy Lee for
helping conceptualize the book at the beginning, to Anita Palmer
for her impeccable work editing the manuscript, and to Ned
and Leslie Bustard for believing in the project.

About the Anselm Society

Based in the Rocky Mountains of Colorado, the Anselm Society's mission is a renaissance of the Christian imagination.

What is a Christian imagination? Put simply: someone with a Christian imagination has learned how to see *heaven in the things of earth,* and *eternity in the things of time.* Through ancient stories and traditions, the Anselm Society exists to help Christians rediscover this calling. To remember who they are; to cultivate a deep awareness of their relationship to the Great Story; and to bring that awareness home to their families and churches.

In our work with artists in particular, we've been struck by the dearth of resources that comprehensively and compactly explain the relationship between God as Creator, the material world He made, and how we relate to both as the image of God. So we approached some of our favorite people and asked if they'd help us make that book. And we were honored when our friends at Square Halo Books agreed to partner with us on it.

Learn more about the Anselm Society and become a member at AnselmSociety.org.

More books about

CREATING

NAMING THE ANIMALS: AN INVITATION TO CREATIVITY
"Naming the Animals is everything one could ask for in a representation of what is good, true, and beautiful. It is a rare offering served with common kindness, accessible language, evocative visual art, and the abiding presence of the unseen God."—Lancia E. Smith

IT WAS GOOD: MAKING ART TO THE GLORY OF GOD
IT WAS GOOD: MAKING MUSIC TO THE GLORY OF GOD
IT WAS GOOD: PERFORMING ARTS TO THE GLORY OF GOD
What does it mean to be a creative individual who is a follower of the creative God? The *It Was Good* books seek to answer that question through essays which offer theoretical and practical insights into artmaking from a Christian perspective.

TEACHING BEAUTY: A VISION FOR MUSIC & ART IN CHRISTIAN EDUCATION
"Teaching Beauty is a must-read for school administrators, teachers, education majors, and all who seek to encourage the next generation to engage in creativity and beauty."—Robert Bigley

LIFTING THE VEIL: IMAGINATION AND THE KINGDOM OF GOD
"A small treasure-house of beauty and imagination, helping us in turn to imagine God's world and God's love with multi-faceted and grateful wisdom."—N. T. Wright

SQUAREHALOBOOKS.COM